Embracing the Now

Finding Peace and Happiness in What Is

Embracing the Now

Finding Peace and Happiness in What Is

Gina Lake

Endless Satsang Foundation

Endless Satsang Foundation

www.radicalhappiness.com

Cover art: © Sam Blight: sam@rangsgraphics.com
www.rangsgraphics.com.au

ISBN: 978-0-6152-4068-8

Copyright © 2008 by Gina Lake

CONTENTS

PART 2 The Ego

PART 3 Breaking Free of Conditioning

(PART 3 Continued)

PART 4 Secrets to Happiness

PART 5 Trusting Life

PART 6 Making the Most of the Moment

About the Author

ACKNOWLEDGMENTS

This book would not have been possible without the help of my inner teacher. It is the result of a collaboration between the wisdom of this teacher and my knowledge, training, understanding, and experience.

INTRODUCTION

This book is a collection of essays that, for the most part, came out of my one-on-one work with others. As I worked with them to help heal emotional issues and awaken, I found the need to address issues more thoroughly that were only touched on in my earlier books. Because the book is made up of essays, it is organized in parts rather than chapters. As a result, it lends itself to contemplation of one essay at a time and doesn't need to be read in any particular order, although it has an intentional order.

Introducing some terms might be helpful, in case this is the first book of mine you've encountered. The terms I've used in this book and my others are very similar to those that Eckhart Tolle, bestselling author and spiritual teacher, has used in his books, *The Power of Now* and *A New Earth*. In those books, he introduced the term *the Now* to refer to the present moment. He also introduced the term *egoic mind*, which is the aspect of the mind that serves the ego, or the false self. *The ego* is the sense of being a *me* and all the ideas, beliefs, and other conditioning entailed in the sense of existing as an individual. The ego is called the false self because the ego isn't who we really are, although it seems like it is who we are.

The egoic mind, which is a reflection of the ego and its conditioning, is the chatterbox mind, which produces a nearly constant flow of commentary about life based on our conditioning. We experience it as *the voice in the head*, as Eckhart Tolle calls it. For simplicity, I sometimes refer to the egoic mind as *the mind.*

However, the egoic mind is distinct from *the functional mind,* which is the aspect of the mind that we use to read, calculate, analyze, design, follow instructions, and so forth. We need the functional mind, but we don't actually need the egoic mind to function.

In writing about the ego, I have somewhat positioned it as the enemy, as a device to help people detach from it. When people are identified with the ego, they are, in a sense, in love with the egoic mind, and I'm hoping to help them fall out of love with it, because the ego and the thoughts and feelings it produces are the source of human suffering. Of course, even the ego belongs to the Oneness, and the ego serves exactly the function the Oneness intended.

The ego isn't actually an entity. Rather, it is the *sense* of being a separate individual, which is innate to us. We feel like individuals, although we are actually manifestations, or expressions, of One Being. This is the Oneness that mystics throughout time have realized as being behind all life and which the term *non-dual,* which means *not two,* refers to. While encased in a human body, we have lost awareness of our true nature, and we are meant to rediscover the truth. That discovery is what the spiritual path is all about and what spiritual practices are meant to reveal.

The sense of being a separate individual is accomplished through the mind. We are programmed to *think* of ourselves as separate and as having distinct characteristics and labels: "I am a man," "I am smart," "I am a mother," "I am twenty years old." Anything that comes after "I am," defines us, and we take those definitions as who we are. And yet when you examine those assumptions, you see that they are just ideas. There is no *you* behind the thoughts about you. This *you* that you think you are is made up of thoughts! What a revelation that is!

Then who are you? That is the perennial question, which ultimately results in the discovery that we are not a *thing* but more of a being, an experience of existing. If we strip away all labels and ideas, we are left with just *I am*, just existence. We are that which is existing right here and now and aware of that existence. Spiritual teachers often call the true self *Awareness* because the experience of the true self is that it is aware. Beyond that, who or what we really are can't be defined. It has qualities that can be felt, such as peace, acceptance, love, compassion, gratitude, kindness, patience, wisdom, and strength, although those words don't come close to defining the mystery of our true nature.

Who we really are is indescribable because it is beyond anything the mind can grasp. But to speak about who we really are, we have to give it a name. It has been given many names: the Source, Spirit, Oneness, Beingness, Consciousness, God, Awareness, the Divine, the Absolute, Presence, Stillness, Emptiness, the Now, Essence, the Self, the higher self, the essential self, and the true self, to name a few. I usually refer to it as *Essence, the Oneness, the Self,* or *Awareness.* Those words mean basically the same thing. I generally use the word *Essence* to refer to the aspect of the Oneness that expresses itself and lives through each of us. Words and definitions are not important. You know Essence when you experience it, just as you know the ego when you experience it. Essence and the ego feel very different and are very distinct.

Awakening is another term that may need some definition. Humanity as a whole is awakening out of the egoic state of consciousness into awareness of its true nature. Many of you are ready to take that step. While someone may have *an awakening,* which forever shifts his or her relationship to the ego, bringing Essence to the forefront, awakening is a process that is never complete. After the momentous shift that is known as awakening, a continued deepening occurs. Before that shift, are more and more experiences of awakeness, until awakeness becomes the constant or nearly constant state. You don't need to understand anything about that process to benefit from this book, which is meant to help you awaken out of the ego and live from Essence.

PART 1

Discovering Who You Are

AWARENESS IS WHO YOU ARE

Awareness always is. There is never a time when we are not aware. Even when we sleep and dream, we are aware we have slept and dreamt. Awareness is the one constant in life. It is even constant after life, for awareness—consciousness—continues even after the body has died, although after death, consciousness is no longer connected to the body. We are what is conscious of life and conscious of everything coming and going. When our attention is placed on consciousness rather than on the comings and goings in life, we feel at peace with whatever is coming and going.

Consciousness, or Awareness, is content with life in whatever way it's showing up. Who we really are is even content to have the experience of an ego that argues with whatever is showing up. Awareness participates in life by being aware of life, but unlike the ego, it doesn't try to control or change life. Awareness just is, and it allows whatever is to be the way it is, for the time being, since life is always changing into something else.

When we are aware of ourselves as Awareness, we have a very different sense of ourselves than when we are aware of ourselves as the ego. When who we are seems to be the ego, we have a specific definition of ourselves: "I am this, not that"; "I am male, not female"; "I am smart, not stupid"; "I am short, not tall." We fit into some categories and not others because the mind defines us in a particular way. In making such distinctions, the mind separates us from others. It makes us distinct from others. That is the egoic mind's job, and it does it very well.

The Awareness that we are, on the other hand, can't be defined. It has no gender, no physical dimensions, no this or that. It is not distinct from anything that is being observed. Although we might experience Awareness as a witness of life, because that's how the mind conceives of it, Awareness is not a witness, but more like *witnessing*. When we are first learning to separate ourselves from the mind, conceptualizing a witness who is observing the mind can be helpful, but that witness is not Awareness. The witness is just an idea that represents Awareness. To witness the mind, we need awareness, but making Awareness into a witness is making it into a thing, which it's not. Awareness is more like the experience of witnessing.

Learning to witness our own mind is the first step in becoming free of the ego and its conditioning. But to free ourselves from identification with the egoic mind takes more than just witnessing the mind. If we witness our mind and still believe it, we are not any freer than when we were identified with it. To be free of our conditioning, we also have to see the falseness of it. Even so, there's one more very important step.

Many people are aware of their egoic mind and the falseness of it, but they still aren't free of it because they are still giving their attention to it. The experience is like watching a bad TV show, acknowledging that it is bad, but staying glued to the TV set. Until we put our attention on what is true instead of on what is false, we won't be free. We will still be experiencing our ego more than our true self.

To be free of the ego requires moving our attention away from our conditioned thoughts to the truth of who we are. It requires knowing ourselves as Awareness and seeing and responding to life as Awareness. When we know ourselves as Awareness, we experience our thoughts as only a small part of what is going on in any moment, not the main show. Awareness takes in all of life, not just what is showing up on the TV screen of our mind. True freedom comes from stepping back from the TV screen of our mind to a place where we can take in the rest of the room and what is going on in the rest of the room.

By becoming aware of what else is showing up in the moment, we can begin to really live in the moment and respond to it naturally, uncluttered by our mental commentary and the ego's desires. We are in the moment without the egoic mind influencing our experience of it. When the voice of the ego no longer dominates and colors the landscape of life, that is spiritual freedom, or liberation. That voice is experienced as one small aspect of the landscape, one other thing that comes and goes in the landscape. The ego's voice becomes impersonal, something in the landscape that has no more personal relevance than a bird's song or the temperature of the room. We still experience it, but we don't experience it as our voice, and we are no longer compelled to follow it or express it.

Once we gain some detachment from the ego's voice, it is possible to experience the Experiencer, the true self, the consciousness that is behind all life and behind our particular life. The Experiencer is in love with life, and when we let it live us, we are in love with life, and our actions and words express that love. Freedom from the ego brings a final relaxation into the true self and the possibility of being that in the world instead of the ego. What a relief!

BECOMING AWARE OF AWARENESS

Becoming aware of ourselves as Awareness is as easy as noticing we are aware. Awareness is so obvious that it's taken for granted, overlooked. Yet, when we turn our attention to what is aware, we get a glimpse of the mysteriousness of who we really are. What is it that is looking out of your eyes and taking in the world? What is looking isn't your eyes. Our eyes are an instrument of awareness, but awareness isn't located inside our head or body, although it seems to be. It's more like awareness is funneled through the body-mind.

At death, awareness is withdrawn, and only the body remains. Then it becomes obvious that whomever or whatever was alive was not the body. Without the animation of the body that consciousness, or the soul, brings to it, the body is just a mass of cells, inert material. When something is said to be soulless, we all know what that means. The soul, although not acknowledged by science, is evident to many who have been with someone as he or she has died.

When the soul incarnates and consciousness, or Awareness, comes into the body, the body becomes capable of being a vehicle for who we really are. The capacity to be aware is Spirit as it lives through what we call our body. We are not actually our body, but the awareness that is operating through it, although we mistake ourselves for the body and for all the other labels given to the body and the personality.

The process of human evolution is a process of dis-identification with the body, mind, and personality and a re-identification with, or a realization of, our true nature. That realization and shift in identification is called *awakening*.

Awakening is the destiny of every human being. Awakening begins by becoming aware of Awareness, by noticing and therefore experiencing more fully what is actually alive in your body. What gives your body life? That is who you really are. You are what brings life into the body and sustains it through breathing and enlivening every system. When the consciousness that you are decides to leave, the body stops being alive.

Who we are is the consciousness that allows the body to be alive and aware. The more we notice Awareness, the stronger the energetic experience that accompanies it becomes. That energetic experience is an experience of aliveness. So although who we really are isn't physical, it can be sensed physically, and it's sensed as vibrational energy, a feeling of aliveness. The energetic sense of aliveness is as close as we can get to experiencing who we really are physically. Becoming more aware of that subtle vibration, or aliveness, helps us align with our true nature.

ALIVENESS

When we are in our body and senses and not in our head, we experience a sense of aliveness that is felt as a subtle energetic vibration, or tingling, and a sense of being alive, illumined, and aware. These sensations are how who we really are is experienced by the body-mind. That aliveness is the felt-sense of who we really are and what we experience when we are in the Now. When we are aligned with who we really are and not identified with the ego, we feel that aliveness, Presence, energetically, and it is very pleasurable.

The fact that who we really are, Essence, can be felt energetically is very handy because it makes identifying when we are aligned with Essence and when we aren't easier. That sense of aliveness can also help us realign with Essence when we are identified with the ego: If you find yourself contracted and suffering, you can search for the sense of aliveness, which is always present, and focus on it. No matter how faint the experience of aliveness is, it will increase as you pay attention to it. Focusing on aliveness is a way of accessing Essence in every moment.

The more you pay attention to the aliveness, the more obvious it becomes. It can become very strong, and when it does, it acts like an anchor, grounding us in the Now and helping us stay there. The sense of aliveness can drown out the ego's mind-chatter, relegating it to the background. If we focus on the aliveness often enough as we go about our day, it will become the foreground, and the mind-chatter will fall into the background.

When we are grounded in aliveness, we experience a deep calm and peacefulness, which allows us to move through our day with equanimity. That peacefulness is unflappable, unless our emotional body gets triggered by some belief or by someone else's belief we've identified with. When that happens, the aliveness is still present and can bring us back into the Now if we give our attention to it rather than to the thoughts and feelings that have been triggered.

Not buying into our thoughts and feelings doesn't make us less human. Being aligned with aliveness instead of our thoughts and feelings is just another way of being in the world. It is not the most common way yet, but a viable and more functional way.

Being aligned with Essence instead of the egoic mind is the next step in humanity's evolution. Eventually we will all awaken out of the egoic mind and live from Essence. Emotions will still exist in potential, but they won't run roughshod over the body-mind. Equanimity, acceptance, and love will be the most common state instead of discontentment, striving, contraction, and fear. Certain individuals are heralding this shift in consciousness and helping to bring it about. The potential to live from Essence exists in everyone, but only some people will choose to make that a priority. The more people who choose it, the easier it will be for the rest of humanity to make that shift in consciousness.

You are probably motivated to make the shift to living from Essence. Paying attention to the feeling of aliveness is one of the most useful tools for awakening. Of course, the egoic self isn't the one who chooses to do that. What chooses to give attention to the aliveness is Essence, as it works to awaken you. The ego will fight that choice all the way. Essence is the awareness of the whole drama between the ego and the *you* that is awakening.

NOTICING AS A DOORWAY INTO THE NOW

The present moment, the Now, is where we meet our true self. Who we really are is not who we *think* we are. Who we really are has nothing to do with thinking and everything to do with not thinking. When we are not involved with the egoic mind, we move into the Now and therefore the experience of who we really are.

The ego, the sense of *me*, disappears as soon as it encounters the Now, so it runs from the Now. It can't survive in the Now. It is revived and survives through thought, particularly thoughts about the past and future, but also through thoughts about the present. The egoic mind tells a story about whatever is happening, and paying attention to these stories takes us out of the Now and into the mind's made-up reality. When we are identified with the egoic mind, we live in the ego's interpretation of reality, not in reality. We live in its explanations about what is, what was, and what will be. These stories take us away from the living reality of the Now.

To experience the Now, we merely have to notice what is happening in the present moment without our interpretations, opinions, judgments, beliefs, or concepts. This may sound difficult, but all it takes is a shift from being absorbed in our thoughts to *noticing* our thoughts. Noticing whatever else is present in addition to our thoughts without interpreting it, judging it, or telling a story about it will bring us into the Now and can keep us there as long as we continue to notice without interpreting or telling stories about what we're noticing. However, once any judgment, opinion, or belief is considered instead of just noticed, we are back in the mind and identified with the ego again instead of with Essence.

Whenever we notice and become fully involved in what *is* without becoming involved in any mental activity, Essence becomes apparent. Noticing is a doorway to experiencing Essence because noticing is a quality of who we really are. Essence is often referred to as *Awareness* because who we are is the Awaring Presence that is conscious and aware of everything. Essence is joyously participating in its creation by being aware of what it has created, including itself manifesting as an individual.

When we stop and ask, "Who am I?" what we find is nothing. We find only Presence, Awareness, Consciousness, which is aware of the thoughts, feelings, sensations, and experiences of the individual that we assume we are. This Awareness, this noticing of everything, is who we really are! Once we realize we are Awareness, the Noticer, it makes sense that noticing is a way back to Essence.

Once we have realized Essence through noticing, allowing is necessary to stay in contact with Essence. Our noticing must be infused with allowing and without any mental activity. Or if there is mental activity, then that is noticed. The ego, on the other hand, does the opposite of allowing. When it notices something, it labels it, judges it, and relates it back to how it will affect *me*. As soon as we become engaged with the mind, allowing stops and resistance takes its place. We become identified, once again, with the *me*, the false self that opposes life, rather than with who we really are.

The Awareness that is our true nature is aware of everything that may be part of any moment: thoughts, feelings, desires, sensations, energy, sights, sounds, inner experiences, intuitions, urges, inspirations, and much more. When we are noticing and allowing, we are also aware of these things. As a result of being aware, a knowing might arise about an action to take. Activity naturally arises from being aware of what *is* in each moment.

The ego has its own experience of each moment and attends to only a small portion of what is possible to experience in any moment. It acts in keeping with its limited perceptions and sense of separateness. These actions are likely to be very different from the actions Essence would take.

Essence allows us to follow the ideas and feelings generated by the ego if doing so doesn't interfere with Essence's intentions, because part of what Essence intends is that we explore the world and create according to our ideas and feelings. Essence is interested in seeing what we will create, but it also has intentions of its own and many ways of guiding us toward those intentions. It also participates in creation by inspiring spontaneous action, action that arises without prior thought.

So you could say there are two types of activity: activity instigated by the ego and activity inspired by Essence. Both are often going on simultaneously. As we evolve, Essence begins to live through us more, and ego-driven activity structures our life less.

Noticing is an important spiritual practice for getting in touch with Essence and with how it is moving us. Essence is very active in our lives and can be more active the more we acknowledge it as a motivating force. The less attention we give the egoic mind and its suggestions for how to live, and the more attention (notice) we give to Essence and its drives and inspiration, the more smoothly and happily we will move through life. Noticing and allowing are key spiritual practices that align us with our true nature and support Essence's intentions for us.

BEING NOBODY AND EVERYBODY

When we are identified with the ego, we feel like somebody: Somebody who likes this and doesn't like that, who wants this and doesn't want that, who looks this way and not that way, who has this history and not some other history, who has certain dreams and desires and not others. All these are woven into an idea and a story about who we are, which makes us feel like a certain somebody. We have an image, a history, goals, and an imagined future. All of this *seems* like who we are. But, as they say, "Things are not always as they seem."

Ideas about what we like, what we've done, what we want, what we look like, and so many other ideas make up our self-image. But our self-image is still just an image, an imagination, a picture, an idea of who we are. It isn't who we really are. Everyone has a self-image, but that doesn't make self-images real. They are just ideas. We pretend we are our self-image and that others are theirs, but no one is an image. Everyone is something other than an image, because an image isn't what is walking around and living life. We also aren't the body we're walking around in. Who we really are is using the body, but it isn't the body.

The problem is that what we really are isn't an image or even a thing. It isn't something the mind can understand because it's beyond the mind and can't be expressed in language. Who we really are is not an image or a thing, but more like an *experience* of no-thing-ness. The mind would rather not acknowledge no-thing-ness because it is uncomfortable with no-thing-ness, since it was designed to deal with things. Because who we really are can't be experienced by the mind, the ego considers who we really are to be nothing, which it is, but not nothing of consequence, which is what the ego assumes.

When we drop out of our mind and into the moment and into our Heart, we experience who we really are, but not as an image. When we are in the Heart (Essence), images and ideas drop away, and what is left is simply an experience of being, or of being nobody in particular: not a male or female, not young or old, not attractive or unattractive, not smart or dumb, not anything we can name. The experience of our true nature is an experience of emptiness. Our true nature is empty of all definition; and yet, it is full and complete, lacking nothing. The experience of being nobody and nothing is equally an experience of being everybody and everything because this emptiness is without boundaries and therefore includes everything; nothing is left out. There's no me and you, but only spaciousness, beingness. That unending spaciousness is who we are.

It's possible to experience nobody-ness or everybody-ness in any moment because our true self is always here—it's what is living life! The reason the empty spaciousness that we are isn't experienced more often or for longer periods of time is that the ego isn't comfortable with it. The ego runs from the experience of who we really are and draws us into its arena—thoughts—where we lose awareness of our true nature.

Whenever you experience who you really are, notice how the ego comes in with a thought to bring you back into its world of ideas *about* life and out of the *experience* of life. Who we are—nobody or everybody—is experiencing life, while the ego just thinks about life and makes up stories about it. What a different reality the ego's reality is than real life! When we give our attention to thoughts, those ideas and beliefs become our reality; and when we give our attention to the experience of the present moment, our true nature becomes our reality.

The more we notice the effect that paying attention to our thoughts has on us—contraction, stress, tension, unhappiness, and negative feelings—the more we will choose to turn our attention away from the world of thought and onto this simple moment. The Now is full and rich and has all the peace we have ever wanted. What the Now doesn't have are the problems and drama created by the ego, which the ego wants because problems and drama keep us attached to our thoughts. Are you ready to exchange your problems and the drama of the ego for peace, contentment, and the experience of being nobody? It's a really good deal.

ACCEPTANCE

Acceptance is a quality of our true nature. The Awareness that we are, Essence, is naturally accepting. It accepts because it loves life— all of life and every possible experience it might have through us. It is so in love with life and with the possibilities that life brings that it embraces even the difficult experiences. It is curious and anxious to experience everything that life (its creation) offers. It jumps into creation with eagerness and joy. We are able to feel that joy if we are willing to. Often we are too caught up in the ego's rejection of life to notice the acceptance and love of life that is the ongoing experience of who we really are.

The ego's resistance to life overshadows Essence's love and acceptance of life until a certain point in our evolution when that shifts. That shift is called *awakening,* and with awakening comes the possibility of loving and accepting whatever life brings. The freedom that comes from spiritual awakening is not freedom from difficult experiences—the same challenges exist after awakening as before—but freedom from seeing a difficult experience as undesirable. Essence loves "undesirable" experiences as much as it loves "desirable" ones, sometimes even more because of their potential for growth.

Acceptance isn't something we can talk ourselves into if we are identified with the ego. The ego has many good reasons for not liking or accepting a difficult experience. Difficult experiences are difficult, after all. Rather, acceptance is something that we notice is already here, however subtle. Acceptance isn't produced by the mind, although it can be obscured by the mind. Acceptance just is. It is unwaveringly here right now and in every moment. Accepting whatever we are experiencing is always possible because who we really are is already accepting it. All it takes to accept something that is difficult to accept is aligning with who we really are instead of identifying with the ego, which is resisting that experience.

One way to align with Essence is to be willing to accept something even if you don't like it. Doing that creates an environment in which aligning with Essence is possible. As long as we are determined to not accept something, which is the ego's usual stance, we will remain stuck in the ego and the suffering it causes. However, a simple statement of willingness to accept what we don't want to accept can free us from being stuck in the ego's resistance to life and open the door for movement toward Essence and acceptance.

To accept what's happening, we don't have to approve of it or like it; we only have to be willing to have the experience we are having *now*. Being willing to have the experience we are having is simply a sane choice, since things can't be any other way than the way they happen to be—for now. Accepting things as they are doesn't mean they won't change, which is the ego's take on acceptance. Accepting things the way they are is simply more functional than not accepting them. Acceptance helps us deal more effectively with whatever we are experiencing. Instead of being lost in fears and negative stories about what we're experiencing, we can be present to the situation, and when we are, we find ourselves responding naturally and wisely to it.

The ego fights to change whatever it doesn't like because, to the ego, life is all about getting what it wants and avoiding what it doesn't want. The ego doesn't see life as having an inherent wisdom and reason for being, beyond avoiding pain and getting more pleasure and whatever else it wants. It also doesn't see life as a process of evolution.

Behind whatever we are experiencing, is a wisdom and purposefulness. When we say yes to it, we are able to align with that purposefulness and find fulfillment in it. Every experience is an opportunity to grow, learn, evolve, and become wiser and more loving, which is how Essence views life.

Acceptance allows us to tap into the potential for good that an experience holds. It allows us to benefit from an experience and move through it as gracefully as possible. And it allows us to feel the joy Essence feels in having that experience and every other experience. Acceptance aligns us with Essence's plan and the role that an experience is playing in our plan so that we can grow from it, as Essence intends.

If you are having difficulty accepting something, acknowledge any resistance and confusion you might be having and affirm that you are willing to have that challenging experience. Then ask for help in accepting the experience, learning from it, and moving gracefully through it. Then if you can, try to align with Essence's perspective of that challenge by being very present in the moment. The peace, joy, acceptance, and wisdom of Essence are always available when we are willing to tune in to Essence instead of focusing on the ego's resistance and complaints. Acceptance is the antidote to the ego's resistance to life and the way out of the suffering created by that resistance.

JUST BEING

Just be. That sounds simple enough. How can we do anything other than be? Being is not something we do, which is what makes just being challenging in our culture of doers. Being is not particularly respected among egos. We have to be *somebody*, and the way we get to be somebody is by doing: You are somebody who has done this or that. The person and persona are created by doing, not by being. However, when all the accomplishments and labels are stripped away, all that's left is a sense of being, of existing, in this simple moment. Such an experience of pure being is the gift that happens just before death for some people, but it can be our ongoing experience.

In the state of pure being, the sense of *me*, or ego, drops away, which is why the ego runs from this state. The ego is striving to be special, not annihilated. Striving is what the ego does. It is always seeking to set itself apart from others in order to be safe or special. When we stop striving, for once, and just allow ourselves to *be*, we find what we were looking for all along: peace and contentment.

Isn't peace and contentment what our striving has always been about? If it hasn't been for peace and contentment, then what has it been for? It has been for everything the ego wants: specialness, comforts, money, possessions, pleasures, safety, and security. We desire these things because they promise to relieve us from the ego's stressful striving and fears. We work so hard in service to the ego's desires, and still we don't find peace and contentment, even when we attain what we desire.

What a surprise it is to discover that we have never needed to strive to survive and be happy after all. Like Dorothy in *The Wizard of Oz*, who discovered that she always had the means for going home, we already have what we need to be happy and safe. We have never really left Home. However, if we don't believe we already have what we need to be happy and safe, it's as if it isn't true: If we don't know that the ruby slippers will take us home, it's like not having them. The ego keeps us from seeing the truth about those ruby slippers—it keeps us from seeing the truth about life. Home is right here, right now, but we may not realize that and therefore not experience Home, or Essence, as much as we might.

The good news is that no matter how lost we might be in striving, there are moments when we experience the peace and happiness that are at our core. The experience may be very fleeting, and we might not think much of it because it isn't what the ego wants, which is something flashier. But peaceful moments spring up unexpectedly even in the busiest day. Briefly, we touch into the radiant and exquisite truth of our being. And then it's gone, like a dream, and we are back in the illusion of the false self and its fantasies of what it needs to be happy.

We can make room for more experiences of radiance, peace, and beauty; and when we do, they arrive. When we make an intention to experience peace, when we value peace enough to make room for it and invite it into our busy lives, it arrives bearing gifts.

We make room for this guest, not by *doing* anything, but by just being, just allowing ourselves to rest, once and for all, in this sweet moment with no agenda, no purpose, no reason but to just experience the moment as it is. We make room for peace and happiness by just noticing them. We notice that they are already here, and noticing them brings them into focus more strongly. Peace and happiness are always here, but they often go unnoticed.

To experience peace and happiness, all it takes is noticing. And noticing is easy. It's our nature to notice, to be aware. It's just that most of the time what we are aware of is our thoughts. Being aware of what's going on outside our head takes nothing more than turning our attention away from thoughts about *me* and onto what is real.

What is real is life, as it exists beyond thoughts about *me* and beyond all the ego's evaluations and commentary. When we notice real life, when we step into the fullness of the Now without thought, we discover peace, contentment, and happiness, an ordinary simplicity that is beautiful and joyful. The experience of peace and happiness is the experience of the real you that is living this life.

AWARENESS MEDITATION

Meditation is such an important practice because it acquaints us with Essence and trains us to move out of our mind. The state of ego-identification is reinforced whenever we believe the egoic mind and the feelings it generates. When we buy into the ego's perceptions, the ego is strengthened. To discover that other perceptions and another way of life exist, we have to turn away from the mind, which has been so empowered by the attention we have given it.

Breaking the pattern of paying attention to the egoic mind takes commitment, and the ego will fight us every step of the way. It resists by balking at meditation, telling us that meditation won't help or isn't helping, that it's too hard, that we don't like it, or that we don't have time. The ego digs up excuses for not meditating.

When we do meditate, the ego chats incessantly at us. It also stirs up fears about what we might experience during meditation and how that might change our life. The dissolution of the ego that happens in meditation can feel frightening, but that fear is natural. Fear is what the ego uses, and always has used, to control us. The ego is only open to meditation because of the possibility of having a spiritual experience that would feel good and make it feel special. If special experiences aren't happening, the ego won't stay interested in meditation.

There is no good reason not to meditate and every reason to meditate. Meditation is the most important thing you can do to support awakening. For most people, a practice of meditation or something similar is necessary to awaken.

A practice of meditation doesn't have to be complicated. It is as simple as anything can be. What's difficult about meditation is committing time to it daily. The regularity of meditation is important to counteract the reinforcement we are habitually giving the egoic mind by being so involved with it.

Something else very important happens when we commit ourselves to a practice of meditation: Spiritual forces that are assisting our evolution are summoned. Affirming our desire to awaken and backing it up with a practice of meditation sends a clear signal to nonphysical forces that we are ready to awaken, and they take it as a cue to help us wake up.

Meditation is as simple as just sitting and noticing, or being aware of, what is occurring—what is coming into our senses, what thoughts and feelings are arising, what intuitions or inspirations are arising, what drives and urges are arising, and what energetic sensations are being experienced—without getting involved in the mind's commentary about these things. Getting us involved in its commentary is how the ego takes us out of the Now. If we dialogue with it or follow its train of thought, we will no longer experience the fullness of the Now, but only a small slice of it.

The goal of meditation is to experience our true nature, or Essence, and Essence is the noticing, aware Presence that we imitate when we sit down to meditate. In imitating Awareness by being aware of everything we are experiencing in the moment (but not identifying with it), we *become* that Awareness, we drop into it. Noticing without getting involved in any thoughts about what we are noticing aligns us with Essence.

When we are aligned with Essence, our experience of the moment changes. Our boundaries soften, we may feel a sense of expansion, and the sense of *me* falls into the background or disappears altogether. Peace, contentment, acceptance, gratitude, compassion, love, and any number of other positive qualities may arise. These qualities are indications of Essence. When we give our attention to those qualities, the experience of them increases.

It's possible to achieve quite a blissful state by meditating, although that's not the goal. The goal is not to achieve a particular good feeling, but to discover Essence and what it intends. Essence is here, living through us. It has chosen to incarnate through our body-mind, and it intends to have certain experiences and accomplish certain things through us. It doesn't push us like the ego, but it inspires us through joy to involve ourselves in certain activities. In meditation, we feel Essence's joy in being alive through us, and we may receive guidance intuitively, which will bring fulfillment if we follow it.

We find peace and contentment in meditating and a welcome respite from the ego's world of striving. We also find true motivation. Meditation brings us into the Now, where we can discover how Essence is moving us. When the mind is out of the way, Essence can guide us more easily. Meditation is far from an escape from life, which is what the ego thinks. Instead, it allows us to align more truly with the life we were meant to live.

WHO CREATES YOUR REALITY?

We are an expression of the Oneness, or Essence, and it creates through us in two ways: It inspires and moves us to create the reality it intends for us, and it also allows our ego to create the reality the ego chooses. So two things are going on in any moment: Essence is attempting to move us in keeping with its intentions, and the ego is attempting to move us in keeping with its desires, beliefs, and other conditioning. In any moment, we have the freedom to choose to follow the ego or to follow Essence.

The ego has quite an advantage because we are programmed to believe we are the false self. In addition, we are programmed to believe the ego's beliefs and desires are ours and that they are true and useful guides for how to live our life. That setup leads to a lot of learning and growth for the character we are playing, and the ego and the programming were created to do exactly that. Our programming, or conditioning, was designed to bring the Oneness a unique experience, because each of us has different programming, and so we are bound to have different experiences.

The Oneness is having this experience through us because creating life is its way of playing, exploring, and expanding itself. It experiences life through us, and it also affects life through us. It shapes life to create the experience it wants by inspiring us to take action and by communicating to us intuitively. When we're not following our thoughts, we discover that we still speak and act in the world. Our thoughts don't determine all our speech and actions, although they determine most of them when we are identified with the ego. When we are identified with Essence, our speech and actions come from Essence, not the ego, and that creates a very different life and experience than when we follow our thoughts.

Thoughts are powerful creators of reality. What we believe often becomes a self-fulfilling prophecy. For instance, if you think you are competent, you will feel confident, and that will help you behave competently when faced with a task. You'll be determined to prove you are competent because that is your self-image. On the other hand, if you believe you are incompetent, you won't feel confident, and insecurity about your capabilities is likely to undermine your will to be competent. We don't like to have our beliefs proven false, even our negative ones. On an unconscious level, we'd rather prove that our negative beliefs are true than change them.

So our thoughts are powerful, but they are only one aspect of our reality and of what is creating our reality. Other people's thoughts and actions also affect our reality, and we have only so much influence over those. More importantly, Essence is guiding our life, and it affects our reality in any number of ways, primarily through our intuition and by inspiring us to take action. Essence is also influencing other people's actions and choices in the same way. Many forces are at work in the creation of our reality: our will, other people's will, and Essence's will.

The Oneness is an active participant in life through its ambassador to life: Essence. The Oneness didn't create us and then leave us to do whatever we wish. It co-exists within us, as Essence, along with the ego, which is just the sense that we are an individual that is separate from other creations and from the Oneness. In reality, there is no separation between ourselves and others and the Oneness because the Oneness has manifested everything and lives through everything. It is playing in third dimensional reality by creating the character that we think of as ourselves and by inspiring and moving this character to act in certain ways. The Oneness, via Essence, is ever-present and active in our life.

We co-create our reality with Essence. We co-create by choosing to follow our desires and thoughts or by following our intuition and the spontaneous movement of Essence as it lives through us. All the while, everyone else has the same freedom of choice, which makes for a very unpredictable, but delightfully chaotic, set of circumstances for Essence (and us) to enjoy.

TWO KINDS OF DESIRES

Desires make the world go around. We desire something, and then we do something about it. Everyone is busy doing something about their desires. Everyone is trying to get what they want. But where do our desires come from? And are they worthy of our time and energy? There are two kinds of desires, and one is not particularly worthy of our time and energy and the other is. One kind of desire comes from the ego, and the other comes from Essence.

The ego's desires can serve Essence, in the sense that Essence wants experience, and it wants to evolve. Pursuing what our ego wants brings us experiences and challenges that evolve us. However, the ego's desires can interfere with certain intentions that Essence has for our life. For instance, the ego often makes choices that lead to money and power, and those choices may interfere with Essence's intentions. Essence may be moving us to pursue something that doesn't result in wealth or power, but in something else it values more.

Essence's intentions aren't always different from the ego's, and when they aren't at odds, we feel little internal conflict. Some of the confusion and conflict we feel around decisions comes from the ego wanting something different from Essence, although the ego often has contradictory desires as well. Contradictory desires or drives arise simultaneously sometimes, and when that happens, we have to choose between them. Following the ego's desires instead of Essence's will be the less satisfying choice, but we may not realize that our choice won't be fulfilling until we meet the consequences of that choice. Life is often a series of corrections: We choose something, and then change course after discovering that wasn't what we really wanted.

What Essence wants usually triumphs eventually because we feel its intentions so strongly and deeply. What interferes with following our Heart the most is our conditioning and other people's conditioning. When we are very attached to our conditioning, including our fears, we often make choices that aren't aligned with Essence, which we later regret. Even then, if our conditioning is strong, we still might not choose differently. Not following our Heart is the source of a lot of suffering and unhappiness.

Fears are what keep most people from following their Heart. Fears go hand and hand with desires. For instance, we *want* security and comfort, so we are *afraid* to follow our Heart, in case being true to ourselves won't provide the security and comfort we want. We also may choose what is familiar just because it's familiar and because we fear the unknown so much that we are unwilling to try something new. This, unfortunately, is the story of many people's lives. Even so, no life is ever a waste, as something is learned from every choice. However, much more happiness and fulfillment can be had from choices aligned with Essence than from ones that come from fear.

Essence allows us to choose the ego's desires over the Heart's for as long as we wish. Most people live many lifetimes before they have enough trust in life (Essence) and enough detachment from the ego to follow their Heart. Eventually everyone learns to be true to themselves. Once we see there is something to choose between— the ego or Essence—then we are very close to living from Essence.

Nevertheless, in everyone's life, there are turning points, or times of transition, when change is called for, and the unknown feels quite scary, no matter how much we've followed our Heart up until then. During times of change, the ego gets very stirred up, and fears can become a real barrier to moving into something new. Once we realize that all fears are produced by the ego, it becomes easier to dismiss them and not allow them to shape our choices.

What does Essence want? The answer lies in the feeling of joy. Whatever Essence wants feels joyful, like a big "yes." Discriminating between the ego's desires and Essence's isn't as difficult as you may think because Essence's intentions show up as joy rather than as a thought. They are known intuitively, or they may pop into our mind as an "Aha," which feels very different from our usual thoughts. Ideas inspired by Essence are accompanied by joy and excitement, while the ego's desires often make us feel contracted, since they come from a sense of lack.

We are meant to co-create with Essence, but we are free to co-create with the ego. Most people go back and forth between the two. At some point in our evolution, however, we want more than anything to be done with the ego's desires and to follow our Heart. That desire comes from the Heart when it is time to awaken. Then life can be lived much more happily and peacefully.

FOLLOWING YOUR HEART

There is little need to define what "follow your heart" means. Everyone knows what it means. Although the Heart is so subtle and so unlike the mind, people are aware of it, and many do honor it. The benefits of following the Heart are, no doubt, quite obvious to you in your life and in other people's lives. Still, trusting the Heart can be hard at times. The mind can be so noisy and instill so much fear that seeing past it to what the Heart is saying and trusting that can be challenging.

The ego's voice is one of fear and distrust. It doesn't trust life. It expects difficulties at every turn and tries to avoid them through planning, speculation about the future, and rehearsals of the future. However, the truth is that such thoughts are impotent. They don't protect us from life, and they certainly aren't capable of predicting the future. They keep us busy in our heads and result in nothing of value.

Despite the impotence of the egoic mind, we trust it. It's a familiar old "friend." But when we look closely, we discover that the egoic mind isn't much of a friend. It often scares us and belittles us until we feel compelled to listen to it. It convinces us that we can't trust life, that we are silly to do so, and that it has the answers to life. We trust the egoic mind out of habit, without examining whether it's trustworthy or not.

When we observe the egoic mind, we discover just how untrustworthy it is, although most people don't examine or question their thoughts. The egoic mind causes us to make poor choices and to feel negatively about ourselves, others, and life. And we don't see that our own mind has done that. That's how strong the programming is around believing it. We really trust it, without question. When we begin to question our thoughts, however, the whole house of cards collapses. How is it we didn't see this sooner? Indeed. The programming is tricky. That's the thing about programming—we aren't supposed to see through it!

The problem is not only that we so thoroughly trust the egoic mind, but also that the ego so thoroughly distrusts everything else, especially Essence. We are programmed to look to the egoic mind for answers and to distrust answers coming from anywhere else. Ultimately, that is not a problem because Essence eventually comes to the forefront and begins to guide our life more. The ego can't perpetuate its ruse indefinitely. Eventually the jig is up, and we see the truth about the egoic mind.

Even those who are still deeply enmeshed in ego-identification act out of Essence many times a day. Essence breaks through even into the most contracted states. It rescues us from entrapment in the egoic mind many times daily. Because Essence is present in everyone, it is possible even for those who are very ego-identified to live a fulfilled life, although they are bound to suffer in the midst of it. Everyone follows their Heart to some extent. We can't help but follow it because we are the Heart. Our programming can only keep us from it so much. That's very good news.

Following the Heart is the only trustworthy choice, really. Trusting the Heart may seem difficult, but once you see how untrustworthy what you have been trusting actually is, then trusting the Heart becomes much easier. Has following your Heart ever failed you? Everyone has had experiences of following the Heart.

What happened when you did? Yes, it was probably scary (and exhilarating), and doing so didn't mean everything went smoothly and exactly as your ego wanted (Does it ever?). But what we discover when we follow our Heart is that the challenges we meet are rich, and the resources we need to deal with them show up. Following the ego's desires and plans by no means guarantees getting what the ego wants either; it's only the *belief* that following the ego's plans will get us what we want that makes trusting the ego easier. What if you believed in the Heart as much as you believe in the ego?

THE SIMPLEST MEDITATION

Here is the simplest meditation, which you can do anywhere and anytime. It is meant to become a way of life, not just a meditation: Notice, without getting involved in any thoughts about what you are noticing. Ignore all of the mind's commentary. Notice not only what is obvious, such as what you are seeing, but also what is more subtle, such as your inner experience and state, your energy and sense of yourself (is it expanded or contracted?), any knowing or intuitions, any drives or motivations, and any thoughts or feelings. Notice not only what's coming in through your senses, but also the impact that has on you subtly and not so subtly. Notice everything that is arising in the moment and being experienced. And if you are involved in doing something, really notice that. There's a lot to notice in any moment!

The reason for meditating is to develop the ability to stay present to thoughts and feelings, which are products of the ego, rather than identify with them. We habitually identify with the egoic mind—we believe our thoughts and feelings—and this causes a lot of suffering. The ego isn't wise, and it keeps us from accessing true guidance and from recognizing what is really living our life. Through noticing, awareness of the Noticer is strengthened. Another name for the Noticer is Essence. The Noticer is who we really are. We are what is noticing, or aware of, life.

This simple meditation helps us get in touch with what we are actually always doing: noticing. However, when we are identified with thoughts and feelings, we lose awareness of the Noticer, which is still there, of course. Getting to know ourselves as the Noticer instead of the egoic mind is what spiritual practices and meditation in particular are all about. Spiritual practices are meant to bring us an experience of Essence. What we are isn't something in another dimension or apart from us; it's right here, noticing the letters on this page. Who do you think is reading this? That which is alive and conscious is reading this, and that is who you really are. Who we really are isn't hidden and apart from life, but engaged and embodied in it.

We are programmed with a sense of being a *me*, with certain desires, thoughts, and ways of being in the world. But who we really are is what is able to notice our desires, thoughts, and tendencies. We are programmed to think we are the *me*, but we are actually what is aware of and can contemplate the *me*. Moreover, we are what can choose to do what the *me* wants or not. Once we're no longer identified with the *me*, we can choose how the *me* will express itself in the world. The *me* doesn't have to be run by the ego, which tends to make negative and selfish choices.

Once Essence takes over, and your choices come from it rather than from the ego, life goes much better. The simple act of noticing is one of the most powerful things you can do to transform your life because noticing moves you out of ego-identification and into Essence.

MEDITATING ON WHAT IS

Meditation is the practice of keeping our attention focused on something that is coming in through our senses: the feeling of air moving in and out as you breathe; movements of energy in your body; a mantra, music, or other sounds; a candle flame, a mandala, something else of beauty, or a picture of a guru. The practice is to bring your attention back to these sensory experiences whenever you find yourself caught up in a thought. When you notice you are thinking, gently bring your attention back to what you are focusing on.

The purpose of this practice is not only to feel peace, but also to train ourselves to be more permanently in our senses and in the experience of the moment rather than in the mind and its version of reality. For most people, meditation provides temporary relief and respite from life and from the mind. However, with a regular and dedicated practice of meditation (an hour or more a day), the effects of meditation spill over into everyday life and influence how we experience life and how we are in life. That's wonderful news and a very good reason to practice meditation.

Nevertheless, meditation can be much more than something we practice once or twice a day. Every moment can be a meditation by learning to be present to whatever we're doing or whatever is going on. Being present is a matter of attending to our sensory experience and not becoming involved in the mind's commentary about that or about something else. As with meditation, being present to life is a matter of getting fully involved in whatever you are experiencing and bringing yourself back to that experience whenever you get caught up in a thought.

Functional thought has a place in our day, of course. We need our minds to read, calculate, study, plan, write, drive, design, and do all the other things we do in our busy lives. The thoughts we don't need, and the ones that meditation and being present train us to ignore, are the ones about *me* and how it's going for the *me*. These thoughts belong to the egoic mind (the ego-driven, or chatterbox, mind), not to the functional mind. The egoic mind, which brings us out of the experience of the moment with evaluations, judgments, stories, fears, doubts, and ideas about the past and future, is not functional, but dysfunctional. It draws us out of the experience of life and into its story about life, which is a place of dryness, contraction, discontentment, and unhappiness. The ego is an unhappy and negative self. Fortunately, it is the false self and therefore unnecessary.

Learning to be present to what *is* and stay present to that takes a lot of practice. All our lives we've been practicing giving our attention to the egoic mind, so it takes some effort to neutralize this habit. Detaching from the mind isn't easy and requires a lot of diligence, but the alternative is quite unpleasant! People often don't realize there is an alternative to listening to the chatterbox mind, but there is: Something else is living life, and the egoic mind just chatters away, pretending it's the one in control. The ego isn't who we really are, although it pretends to be, and it isn't in control, although Essence allows us to follow the egoic mind if we choose.

The more accustomed we become to being present, the more we begin to live as Essence, which is a free and joyful experience. The

Now is not only a place of sensory experience, although that is sufficiently rich, but also where life comes out of. If we aren't paying attention to the Now, we might miss what life is trying to bring about through us. We can follow the egoic mind's plans and ideas for our life if we want to, but something else right here and now has a plan, and that plan will be much more satisfying than anything the ego has to offer.

ALIGNING WITH ESSENCE

We are actually already aligned with Essence because we are Essence! We can't be anything other than Essence, but we are under the illusion that we are the roles we play and the ideas we have about ourselves. The *I* that we think of ourselves as is just the idea *I*. Like every other concept, the *I* has no objective reality. The idea *I* gives us a sense of existing separately from others and from the rest of life, but the *I* is just the thought *I*. Sit with this revelation a moment. Your sense of self is derived from a set of ideas about yourself, which came from others and from conclusions you drew about yourself because of your experiences.

The *I* is so adorned with images, beliefs, opinions, desires, fears, and feelings that it can be difficult to see that these, too, are just ideas, or stem from ideas. We have quite a complete image of ourselves in our mind, and people reinforce each other's self-images. The experience of our body as a boundary between ourselves and other people completes the picture of who we think we are. We believe we exist within the limits of our body. It does seem that way, but we don't actually exist within that boundary or in any particular location. Rather, our soul, or spirit, gets assigned to a body-mind, and we take that body-mind as who we are.

Aligning with Essence is a matter of realizing that we are not the body-mind we are functioning through but the essence of life itself, poured into, if you will, a particular body-mind. The essence of life that we are doesn't fit inside one body-mind, so our body-mind is hardly a complete representation of who we really are. We are squeezed into this container, which shapes and limits our expression. The container is that of a human being (at least this time around!). We are just playing at being a human being, and we have played at being a human being in many other lifetimes. We are learning certain lessons that belong to this particular life form. We will also go on to experience other forms, including nonphysical forms.

The mind isn't designed to comprehend the truth about who we really are, nor is it designed to believe the truth. Nevertheless, a part of us does know the truth and resonates with the sense of being much vaster than we seem to be. That larger sense of ourselves is what calls us Home.

The experience of our true nature is always available, since Essence has never been anything but here all along. There is nowhere we have to get to, to be aligned with Essence. Aligning with Essence is not something we do. It happens more as a result of allowing and noticing what we already are and suspending our belief that we are who we *think* we are.

When our thoughts stop or are not given attention, Essence shines through. Thoughts temporarily obscure, or cloud, the experience of Essence, but Essence is always there, aware of the character it is playing and all the thoughts that character is having. Essence is aware of the beliefs, opinions, fears, dreams, feelings, desires, and judgments of this character, and Essence allows it to have these thoughts and do what it will do with them. When the actor begins to wake up out of the role that he or she has been playing and glimpses the truth, the truth propels him or her on the spiritual path. Aligning with Essence is a matter of turning our attention in every moment to our true nature rather than to the illusory false self. We wake up out of the dream of the false self into the reality of our true nature. What a dream it has been!

GOING DEEPER INTO ESSENCE

Being in our senses brings us into the Now. When we really take in what we are seeing, hearing, feeling, and tasting without becoming involved in our mind's commentary about it, we are in the Now. But there's much more to being in the Now than sensory experience. Our senses are only a doorway into the Now. The joy of being in the Now goes beyond the pleasure of the senses. To go deeper into Essence, there's another very important step, once we are fully sensing without the interference of the mind's commentary, and that is to fully experience the *effect* that sensory experience has on our Being.

When you look at a beautiful flower or hear a bird sing, what impact does that have on your internal, energetic experience? What is your Being experiencing? Or another way of asking this is, what is Essence's experience of that? Just take a moment and discover what Essence is experiencing for yourself. Look at something beautiful. Really take it in and notice how beauty makes you feel, not emotionally, but energetically within your being.

When we really take in beauty or anything else we are experiencing through our senses, we feel our Being celebrating and rejoicing in the moment, and we experience that energetically. That subtle energetic experience is the experience of the Heart, or Essence. That subtle joy, expansion, relaxation, yes to life is the radical happiness that comes from experiencing life as Essence experiences it.

That subtle experiencing is ongoing and ever-present, but we often don't notice our Being celebrating life because thinking is more obvious and compelling, even though thinking is actually less rewarding. Because thinking is our default position as humans, we have to *learn* to notice what else is present besides thoughts. We have to learn to notice what is real and true. We have to train ourselves to pay attention to the subtle joy, expansion, relaxation and yes of Essence as it enjoys life through us. That subtle experience becomes less subtle and easier to notice the more we put our attention on it rather than on our thoughts. Then the mind becomes quieter, softer, and more in the background.

Since the egoic mind is the generator of all suffering, it's really good to know that it doesn't have to be prominent and that something else that is much truer and more pleasant can take its place. Our Being, Essence, is happy in every moment. Just notice that. Notice how your Heart expands when you see beauty, hear a sound, or simply experience what is arising in the moment in some other way. Notice how much you actually love life. Your love for life is always accessible just by noticing it.

PART 2

The Ego

SEEING THROUGH THE *I* THOUGHT

Most of the chatter that comes from the egoic mind is all about *me.* If you notice, you'll see that nearly every thought starts with *I*. Such thoughts define the *I*: "I am," "I like," "I want," "I believe," "I was," "I will be." Who would you be without these thoughts to define you? And where do these definitions come from? Are they consistent, or do they change from day to day?

Some of the definitions of yourself came from others. When we are children, we take on the definitions that others, particularly our parents or other authority figures, give us. We also draw conclusions about ourselves based on our experiences. For instance, if we failed at something important to us, we might define ourselves as a failure.

Where these definitions, or identities, came from and what they are, are not nearly as important as seeing their lack of completeness and therefore their falseness. We can't think a true thought about ourselves (or about anyone else) because nothing we think or say about ourselves is the complete truth, not even the complete truth about our ego or personality, much less about our true self. If you say, "I'm smart," that's true relative to some people only. If you say, "I'm talkative," that's true sometimes, but not always. If you say, "I love motherhood" or "I love ice cream," that may seem absolutely true, but such statements imply you always feel that way. Can you think of one time when such a statement wasn't true or imagine sometime when it might not be? We believe many things to be true of ourselves, but are they really?

Who we really are and even who we think we are is mysterious and can't be captured in words. The ego's definition of itself—it's likes and dislikes, what it believes, and what it desires—is constantly changing. Who are you if you can't be clearly defined? We have *ideas* about who we are, but these ideas change, and some just aren't true. They are assumptions of an identity, a belief that we are a certain way. They are a self-image, an image of ourselves, and that image is in flux.

Rather than being something constant and stable, who we *think* we are is quite inconsistent and not necessarily true. We try very hard to define ourselves, but we never succeed. The ego is made up of beliefs about ourselves that are continually changing. All the ego is, really, is ideas about itself. Such ideas have no substance—they are just thoughts, after all—and they have very little truth. They are entirely subjective.

How valuable can thoughts about *I* be, then? Even when they are positive, they are meaningless. And when they are negative, they can color our experience of life quite dramatically: When you see yourself as flawed or inadequate, life feels bad. But even if your self-image is positive, it won't likely be that way for long. Our self-image has a way of swinging between positive and negative. These polarities are two sides of the same coin, and neither is true. The positive things we say about ourselves are as relative and as inadequate to the task of defining us as the negative things are.

This fact renders all *I* thoughts useless to us. Their only purpose is to create a false identity, and who needs that? Only the ego. Do you need these definitions, these self-images, to function? All along, you have been functioning, and the identities created by your thoughts have just been tacked on. They aren't the reason we are able to function and, in fact, they often interfere with functioning. They color how we see ourselves and create a false sense of self that mediates between the true self and the world. The false self interferes with being in the world more purely and innocently. It affects our experience of the world and influences how we interact with it.

Essence, which spontaneously acts in the world, doesn't need the false self. It allows the false self to influence us because it created the ego to do what it does, but Essence doesn't need the ego to experience life. The false self creates the drama in life and the sense of having a problem. It serves us by providing the grist for the mill of our evolution. But at some point, we are ready to move beyond it, and we no longer need to experience life through its lens. We discover that we have never needed the false self or our *I* thoughts. They don't represent who we really are, and they have never really served us. Such thoughts have only served to create the illusion of a separate self. Once we see that that self is an illusion—just thoughts, really—we can begin to live more from Essence.

The *I* keeps us out of the Now by keeping us involved with it mentally. *I* thoughts keep us from discovering who we really are. Once we see we aren't the *I*, ignoring our *I* thoughts and putting our attention on life becomes much easier. When we believed that our *I* thoughts were true, important, and who we were, we were naturally interested in them and we felt we needed to follow them. Once we see that they aren't true, it is possible to realize what else is here, living life. We discover that what is living life has nothing to do with thought and everything to do with purely experiencing the moment without thought.

THE EGO IS A TROUBLEMAKER

The ego's ongoing state is discontentment. Whatever is happening is either not enough of something or too much of something: not enough pleasure, not enough relaxation, not enough beauty, not enough freedom, not enough comfort, not enough money, not enough power, not enough success, not enough security, too much stress, too much quiet, too much noise, too much solitude, too much socializing. Like the story of the three bears, whatever is happening is hardly ever just right. Even when it is, the ego stresses over the future or regrets the past, and in doing so, can spoil even an experience that is "just right."

The ego supports and feeds its discontentment with a story, explaining what's wrong with the way things are and why things should be different. The ego complains about and judges whatever we are experiencing, which makes it quite unpleasant. A perfectly okay moment becomes not okay because the ego says it's not okay and tells us why. The ego can spoil even the best moments with its negative point of view, complaints, and judgments. It decides it doesn't like something, builds a case against that, and then becomes miserable because it believes its own story. The ego doesn't realize that its story is the problem, not what's going on. And when we are identified with the ego's story, neither do we.

The ego's point of view is often a negative one. The ego is a troublemaker, a maker of drama, not a peacemaker. When we agree with the egoic mind, we feel like a victim or like we have a problem to fix. When we don't agree with it, we just experience the moment as it is, without the ego's negative influence. The negative commentary of the ego may continue, but if we don't agree with its point of view, we just flow from one moment to the next, easily and peacefully, without telling a story about whatever is going on. Life keeps moving on, and we are going with the flow.

Going with the flow is an experience of no *me*. We are not focused on the ego's commentary—"I am...." "I like...." "I don't like...." "I want...." "I wish...."—but on what we are doing or on whatever is happening. We are absorbed in life as it is happening instead of on the *me's* story about whatever is happening or about what happened or will happen. The ego tells a story about what is happening that places itself at the center of the universe. It categorizes every moment as good for *me* or bad for *me*. It judges each moment according to its likes and dislikes and whether the moment meets its desires or not. The ego's story is the beginning of suffering. If we listen to its story, we become identified with its unhappy voice, and that becomes our reality. But if we ignore its story, we stay in the flow of the moment, where we can just enjoy life as it is unfolding.

When we are in the flow, there's no problem. The ego creates problems by defining something as a problem. When we don't listen to its opinions and fears, we don't experience having a problem. We still might have experiences we don't like, but not liking something doesn't have to be a problem unless we decide that what we are experiencing is the wrong experience.

Every experience is the right experience. There's no such thing as a wrong experience. Whatever story the ego tells is one of many possible stories, none of which contains the complete truth. The ego usually tells a negative story, which reflects its values, beliefs, and opinions. Such thoughts don't deserve our attention because they are anti-life, anti-love. They separate us from life and from others, and they lead to unhappiness.

The only opinion about life that is worth holding is that it is good just as it is. That is the "opinion" of Essence, which loves life and loves having whatever experience it is having through us. Any other opinion takes us out of the Now. Once that happens, we are drawn into the ego's world of discontentment, complaints, judgments, and attempts to fix whatever it doesn't like, which is a lot.

You can spend your time trying to create a better *me* and a better experience for the *me,* or you can be fully engaged in the experience you are having. When you allow yourself to relax into the moment, you discover that you never needed the *me* in order to live your life. The *me* is not who we are, but a figment of our imagination, just a set of ideas about *me.* Essence has always been the one living our life, and it has allowed us to pretend to be a *me.* Once we see the uselessness of the *me,* we can just relax and enjoy the moment just the way it is.

TAKING A BREAK FROM THE STORY OF *Me*

To every moment, the ego brings the query: "How's it going for me? How is my story going? Am I getting what I want? Will I get what I want?" The ego is always checking to see if *I* am good enough, if the moment is good enough, if other people are good enough. And they usually aren't. The ego has very high standards, and the moment and life hardly ever measure up, which causes a lot of suffering. *Me* and *my life* are rarely good enough for the ego. The *me* is always striving to be better, to have more, and for its life to look a certain way. We suffer so much over the story of *me* and how well it is going. What a relief it is when we drop into the Now, where there is no *me* and no story about *me*.

From the ego's perspective, life will be good and happy when the ego gets its way, so the ego works very hard to get life to go its way. Unfortunately for the ego, life has its own way of going, and the ego actually has very little to say about how life goes. In spiritual circles, we hear a lot about surrender because surrender is necessary to experience our true nature. What we surrender is the ego's agenda, the *me* project: all the ideas the ego has about what we should be like, what we should achieve, and how our life should look and feel.

We surrender these ideas when we finally see the pointlessness of trying to make ourselves and life fit them. The willingness to surrender them usually happens only after many disappointments in life. For most, the spiritual search begins later in life, after we've tried and tried to make life work out according to our ideas and plans, only to discover that it has its own plan. The suffering caused by this disappointment puts many of us on the spiritual path, wondering what life is about anyway if it's not about getting what we (our egos) want.

The suffering caused by the *me* and by trying to get our story to go right eventually brings us to our knees. When we are willing to surrender our ego's ideas, including its desires, we can experience the moment purely. When we do that, we feel at peace, which comes from the relief of no longer having a sense of being *me* with an agenda. What a relief it is to drop the *me* for even a moment. We actually all experience the dropping of the *me* many times a day. Whenever we feel a quiet contentment with life and an ease of being, that means we have dropped into the Now and lost our sense of *me* and its story of what it wants and needs to be happy.

We think we need our stories. If we didn't have them, we are afraid we would never accomplish anything. We are afraid we wouldn't have a life. But such fears are unfounded. Instead of benefiting our life, our stories (e.g., "I like...." "I want...." "I need...") cause us to suffer over life. Without our stories, life is still here, but the suffering is gone.

We are meant to discover that we can live without our stories and that we don't have to suffer. Suffering is a choice: We can have our story of *me,* or we can just be alive in the present moment and see what happens next and what Essence moves us to do. Life springs out of the Now. We can trust life to do that. Life doesn't need the ego's agenda or its desires for life to happen. When we drop into the Now, we experience the life we are having, without trying to make it be any different than it is. When we are in the Now, we gain everything we have been looking for: peace, contentment, happiness, and love. From the Now, life takes care of itself because we are Life.

THE END OF STRIVING

One of the gifts of terminal illness can be the cessation of striving. When we know that our life will soon be over—when the play we've been starring in is about to come to an end—we stop striving to be someone, get something, and get somewhere. The ego's story is all about being someone special by attaining or achieving something. The ego has a storyline in mind. It knows how it wants the story to go and how it wants the story to end, and it wonders how it will go and end. When all of that striving, dreaming, and desiring no longer make sense because we are about to die, we may be freed from the ego. The cessation of striving that often accompanies terminal illness opens the door to discovering and experiencing more fully who is really here and who has always been here beneath the costume. When our functioning is stripped away, our looks are gone, and possessions no longer mean anything, who or what remains? What a blessing it is to find out the truth about who we are. This discovery is one of the spiritual purposes of terminal illness.

Most of our thoughts are in service to the ego, the *I* that we think of ourselves as. They promote a story about ourselves that is driven by desires and other conditioning: "I have to do that, I should do that, I can't do that, I want that, I need that." This story seems true and real. We believe we need our story to go a certain way, even when life has other plans. So we strive and push against life, trying to make that story happen—and happen on our own timetable. It's natural to do this. However, all this striving and suffering over how our story is going isn't necessary because life is happening anyway, and it is happening as it is meant to be happening, and on its own schedule.

Our ideas about ourselves and how our life is going or should go cause so much unnecessary suffering. Life has a plan, and it will have its way with us. It brings us the lessons we need, which shape us in ways we need shaping, and it brings us the opportunities it intends for us. Our egos are operating within a larger framework, or plan, that the ego is unaware of. When that larger plan is different from the ego's plan, or story, we may suffer greatly. And when the larger plan isn't at odds with the ego's plan, we are at peace with life. We can argue with what life brings us and suffer because life isn't going like our story is supposed to go, or we can see that even that experience is the right experience.

When we are able to see the ego's striving for what it is—a frantic, egocentric attempt to be someone special, to be safe, to be admired, and so on—then we can begin to let go of striving. It is only the ego that needs the things the ego wants. The ego wants what it wants for itself, not for love or a higher purpose. Who we really are has no need of anything, but already has everything it needs to be happy.

Striving is actually what makes us feel lacking, as if we don't have what we need to be happy. We strive because we believe we need something to be happy, when we have never needed anything at all, and nothing "out there" will ever satisfy us anyway. The ego takes us on a wild goose chase. It convinces us that we need to be someone and have our life look a certain way to be happy, and we don't. We don't suffer because we don't have what we want, but because we believe we need something other than what we already have to be happy.

At death, everything the ego has wanted is denied and stripped away, which is why some people discover supreme happiness just before they die. What a relief it is to have the tyrannical ego off our backs! The ego is a tyrant that drives us away from happiness, not toward it. Many people find this out just before they die, but what a blessing it is to discover it even before that! Just by seeing that we don't need what our egoic mind says we need to be happy, we can become free of the ego's domination.

Once we stop following the ego's ideas about what to do, we begin to discover what else is here living our life, silently awaiting our notice. What we truly are is very patient, very loving, very accepting. It patiently waits until we are ready to discover it and discover the peace and happiness it has to offer when we stop trying to be someone and get life to turn out "right." Then who we really are can begin to live through us more fully, which results in the happiness we've been striving for but looking for in the wrong places. Once we begin living as who we really are, we won't be striving anymore. We will be moving through life with fluidity, grace, acceptance, and love. We will be taking action, but acting will be done *through* us. What a paradox it is that we get what we've been striving for only when we stop striving!

THE EGO IS IRRATIONAL

The ego is irrational. Its strategies to change reality don't affect it, but only make us unhappy. Once we see how irrational the ego is and how ineffective its strategies are, we can begin to free ourselves from it and from the suffering it causes. The ego pretends to know how to make us happy, but its strategies produce the opposite and, in fact, obscure true happiness.

One of the ego's favorite strategies for trying to change reality is judging. When we don't like something (i.e., when we are identified with the ego, which rejects the way things are), we judge whatever we don't like. Judging provides reasons for not liking something: It's too this or too that. Or, it's not enough of this or that. Judgments make the ego's discontentment with everything seem reasonable. They provide reasons that justify our complaints and the anger generated by those complaints.

Anger stems from assuming that the ego's perspective is correct and that the ego's desires should be met. What assumes that, of course, is the ego; we don't have to. That assumption is a highly irrational one. Life doesn't revolve around the ego's desires. And infinite perspectives are possible, and every ego has its own. So why should our ego's perspective be the correct one?

The ego's perspective is colored by its values. It wants security, superiority, fame, power, money, safety, comfort, and pleasure above other values, such as love, peace, and unity. As a result, the ego sees the world from the standpoint of how well the world is providing what it wants. The moment is good or bad, depending on whether what is happening makes the ego feel good, safe, powerful, beautiful, comfortable, rich, popular, happy, or whatever else it wants.

When the moment doesn't provide these things, the ego feels cheated and angry. It judges and complains, building a case for its anger so that it feels justified in feeling angry and, perhaps, in taking some destructive action. If the ego's anger took place in a vacuum, it would be obvious how pointless and impotent that anger is. But anger is meant for others to see, because the ego uses anger to try to get its way in the world. The ego tries to manipulate others with anger, and it's often successful, but only at a great cost.

The ego doesn't care about the cost of indulging in anger: a diminishment of love, harmony, and happiness. It cares more about getting what it wants. It wants what it wants more than it wants love or even happiness, because ultimately its choices don't lead to happiness. The ego would rather have its perspective than be happy. When it does succeed in getting what it wants, it gets little out of having that. The victory is a hollow one.

The hollowness of the ego's successes doesn't stop it from continuing to apply its favorite formula to life, which is: Reject something, judge it, complain about it, and get angry or sad about it. The ego actually enjoys feeling angry and sad. When we are identified with it, we enjoy these feelings on some level and often unconsciously choose to stay in them for a while rather than move beyond them. When we choose anger or sadness over happiness often enough, anger and sadness become natural and familiar, like old friends, and those feelings become automatic whenever life doesn't go our way. Fortunately, we can learn to respond differently when things don't go our way, and with a little practice, anger and sadness will no longer be automatic and unconscious.

Anger is an attempt to manipulate life, which is particularly irrational when what we are angry about is something that happened in the past. Being angry at something we think will happen in the future is equally irrational, since the future is just an idea. Being angry at something in the past or future is irrational because being angry doesn't change anything; it only makes us and others unhappy. Being angry at something that is presently happening isn't rational either because anger doesn't help us cope with the present either. Anger simply isn't functional.

When we feel angry, we are actually angry because of a perception we have. We are saying something to ourselves that is making us angry. The story we are telling ourselves is making us angry. If we don't want to feel angry, then we have to stop telling ourselves and others that story. The solution doesn't lie in changing anything outside ourselves, but inside ourselves.

Sadness is a stance of defeat or victimization in relation to life, which also brings only unhappiness and, like anger, has no power to change reality. Sadness, like anger, is also often an attempt to manipulate life and others. We hope that others will come to our rescue and give us what we want if we are really sad about it. Sadness can also be an unconscious attempt to manipulate God into giving us what we want. We throw a tantrum over life in hopes that Daddy/Mommy will finally give us what we want. We make ourselves sad by disagreeing with the way life is showing up, and we hope that life will show mercy on us.

Both of these strategies, anger and sadness, are ineffective ways of dealing with life. They don't change whatever we don't like, and they are harmful to us and our relationships. These feelings are the result of the ego's irrational perspective, which assumes incorrectly that life should conform to its wishes and that it can make life do that, or that it should be able to. The ego believes it is the center of the universe, which is an immature and inaccurate perspective. Spiritual maturity is seeing the truth about life. The ego is immature, irrational, self-centered, and shortsighted, but the good news is that we are not the ego! More good news is that spiritual maturity doesn't depend on our ego changing, but on simply recognizing the truth about it.

When you catch yourself complaining or judging, that means you are identified with the ego's perspective. When you realize that and stop complaining or judging, you will stop suffering. However, stopping in the midst of complaining and judging isn't always easy because the ego loves to complain and judge. But the less we indulge in that negative pleasure, the weaker the ego becomes. Instead of complaining or judging, give your attention to something else: something of beauty, something you love or are grateful for, something you're experiencing through your senses, or your breath. Give your attention to anything but your negative thoughts.

If you find yourself angry or sad, ask yourself what you just said to yourself that made you feel that way. Seeing that you created those feelings by believing your thoughts empowers you to move beyond those feelings. Our feelings are the outcome of believing negative thoughts. Although there may be some truth to such thoughts, which is why we believe them, they are a story we are telling ourselves that leaves out much of the truth. When we feel bad, those feelings mean we have bought into the ego's story about ourselves, our life, or others, and the ego's story is a negative, small, shortsighted, and ignorant one. What story would Essence tell? Essence sees the big picture and the truest perspective. It always has an uplifting story to tell. If you are going to tell a story at all, find Essence's story. Better yet, just be in the moment without any story to distract you.

LIFE IS SPRINGING OUT OF THE NOW

Everything comes out of the Now, the present moment. The present is all that exists, and it's all we have. The past is brought into the present as a memory and a story, and the future is brought into the present as a desire and a fantasy, but neither the past nor the future is real. They are just thoughts. Only the experience we are having right now is real, and the experience of the Now is constantly changing. That's the truth, but the ego doesn't accept it. The ego rejects the Now and wants something different. So it takes us out of the Now with thoughts about the past, thoughts about the future, and evaluations of the present. The ego isn't interested in experiencing the Now because the Now never has enough of what it wants.

The ego wants glamour, fun, excitement, success, attention, power, praise, money, fame, and superiority. Only some moments offer the things the ego prizes so dearly. Most moments are quite ordinary and simple, without a lot of fanfare and specialness for the ego. If a moment doesn't hold something special for it, the ego isn't interested in what it does have to offer. Even when the moment has what the ego wants, it's quick to find fault with that or want even more of that. The truth is that the ego is rarely happy, even when it does get what it wants.

Life is not about ego-gratification, which is why the ego is so unhappy. Life is about experiencing, growing, evolving, creating, serving, and expressing ourselves in the world in a way that is meaningful and aligned with the Whole. The ego doesn't consider the Whole. It experiences itself as separate and on its own. However, what is actually living life, Essence, operates to support the Whole. The actions that Essence takes in the world are meaningful and fulfilling because they are aligned with the Whole, while the actions the ego takes are unsatisfying because they are rarely aligned with it. There is no true happiness in pursuing the ego's goals, although the ego tries to convince us otherwise. We come to see that something else is alive and living our life. Allowing that to express itself through us is far more rewarding than expressing the ego's thoughts and chasing after its desires.

Discovering what Essence intends for us is possible, but we have to be in the Now to find that out, not in our head. The ego uses the mind to direct our life according to its values, while Essence shapes our life by using our intuition and inspiring us to act. When Essence is orchestrating our life, we feel moved to do or say something. We don't think about it; we just do it, and doing it feels right. Essence moves us to create a life that will be fulfilling if we allow it to, that is, if we don't listen to the egoic mind instead.

We have free will. We can choose, in any moment, to pay attention to the mind and follow its values or to pay attention to Essence and follow its values, which are love, compassion, peace, acceptance, growth, wisdom, and understanding. When we put Essence's values above the ego's, we discover the happiness we've been looking for. Aligning with Essence isn't difficult. We just have to be willing to pay attention to something other than the egoic mind. When we do, we discover that we didn't need the egoic mind at all. We discover that life has been happening all along, springing out of the Now, and all the ego has ever done is take us away from the contentment that is available right here and now.

HOW THE EGOIC MIND TAKES YOU OUT OF THE NOW

As soon as we land in the Now, the egoic mind has something to say about it. Sometimes it makes a friendly comment, such as, "This is nice," and sometimes it is critical: "What's so great about this?" At other times, it orders us about: "You need to get to work now" or "Don't forget to do that." The egoic mind is often full of advice or aphorisms: "Be careful!" "A stitch in time saves nine." The mind's commentary accompanies nearly every moment. When that commentary is absent, it can be quite an amazing experience, since it is so rare for most people.

The voice of the egoic mind may be friendly, mean, bossy, wise, or kind. Any kind of communication you have ever experienced will be imitated by the mind. If, as a child, you experienced mostly kindness and generosity, then your thoughts will reflect that. And if you experienced criticism and cruelty, then your mind will be full of that, toward yourself and others.

Most of us experience a mixture of mental voices that vary according to our mood. When we are happy, our mind's voice is likely to be friendly, chatty, and pleasant. When we are tired or stressed out, its voice is more likely to be negative and critical. The voice in our head can also make us feel unhappy, angry, or any other feeling by telling us something that causes us to feel that way. This voice reflects moods and feelings *and* creates them.

The voice in our head also changes according to our relationship to it. If we aren't listening to it as it tries to chat with us, then it might scold us or try to scare us to get us to pay attention to it. The egoic mind doesn't like to be ignored, and it finds ways to involve us with it. If we are on to its negativity and we stop paying attention to it when it's being negative, then it will try to be our friend and attempt to be helpful, interesting, or entertaining. Whatever works is what it will try again. A certain relationship with our mind becomes established that is often repeated until we change that relationship by ignoring that voice.

The egoic mind doesn't have anything useful to say, but we don't know that until we finally see that for ourselves. Even once we realize how worthless the egoic mind is, we may still pay attention to it, just in case it comes up with something useful. Occasionally, something pops into the mind that is useful, like "Don't forget your keys!" Or maybe suddenly we remember where we left our keys. We usually attribute such brilliance to the egoic mind, but these are examples of Essence using the mind to help us.

The egoic mind is like a computer that spits out information, rules, beliefs, and other ideas it has acquired that don't necessarily have much relevance to the present moment. Such ideas may have been true and useful in the past, but they aren't necessarily true or useful now. Essence, on the other hand, releases information and wisdom we need into the present moment. Usually it does this through our intuition, although sometimes what we need to know pops into our mind as a word or a phrase, but never as a lengthy monologue. When information or wisdom pops into our mind, it feels very different from the usual mental commentary. But because the information or wisdom appeared in the mind, we might assume it came from the mind rather than from Essence.

Once you realize how useless the egoic mind is, then Essence will be able to function more effectively through your mind. It will use your mind more, and the ego will use it less. The mind can be a servant of either. If you stop paying attention to the voice in your head, you don't have to worry about losing the ability to think or function. You will function much more effectively and with much more ease and harmony if you don't pay attention to it. And messages from Essence won't get lost in the mind-chatter, as they often do now.

The only thing that can take you out of the Now is listening to the voice in your head. When we pay attention to it, our attention shifts from the real experience of the present moment to the world of thought. Once we are involved in the mental realm, it's easy to get caught up in one thought after another and then in any feelings that are triggered by those thoughts. Paying attention to the egoic mind is a slippery slope. Fortunately, once you see what the mind is up to and are convinced that it doesn't have anything useful to say, you can stay right here in the experience you are having. Then you will discover how beautifully life arises out of the Now—and always has!

FIXING THINGS THROUGH THOUGHT

A lot of our thinking is an attempt to fix things that can't be fixed. For example, we might try to fix the past by trying to do it over mentally, by imagining other ways it could or should have gone, or by trying to defend what we did by thinking about it. We replay the past as if doing so can change it. The mind tries to fix what it cannot fix.

We do a similar thing with the future. We might try to plan something down to the last detail, as if doing so can cause the future to go the way we imagine or want it to go. Although some planning has value, the mind overdoes it, as its planning is often driven by needless worries and fears. The mind runs "what if" scenarios and tries, through thought, to avoid the messiness and unpredictability of life, however impossible that may be.

The mind also spends a lot of time trying to fix things that don't need fixing. It imagines, or anticipates, problems where none exist and, as a result, spends precious energy trying to fix something mentally that isn't even real. For example, you might imagine that you will "fall on your face" while speaking to a group, when that has never happened before. Even if you have had difficulty speaking to a group before, thinking about it in the future can't change what has happened or will happen. Thinking about it is just needless worrying.

The trouble with trying to fix something by thinking about it is that it doesn't work! We can't change the past by thinking about it. And even to learn from the past, we don't need to think about it.

Whatever we learned is already "in our bones." We already just know it. The truth is that we can only "fix," or affect, *real* life—what is happening right now—by *doing* something in the present. We don't affect real life by thinking about it. We can think and imagine all we want, but thinking won't change the past or affect the future or even change what's happening now, because it's already too late to change what's happening *now*.

The other problem with trying to fix something by thinking about it, besides the fact that it doesn't work, is that it affects our experience of the present moment because it takes us out of real life and puts us into our own made-up mental world, which for many people is full of worry, fear, and other negativity. We try to manage and control life through thought, and we are programmed to believe we can, but the truth is we can't. Seeing this is our ticket out of hell and to realizing that life is already fine the way it is and that nothing ever needed fixing.

The egoic mind imagines a problem, and then it imagines a solution. When we get caught up in such thoughts, we feel like we have a problem that has to be solved before we can be happy. But the problem is just imagined! When we drop out of involvement with these thoughts and into the simple experience of the present moment, we discover that everything is fine just the way it is. Life never had to be any different than it is, nor do we. We can be the "imperfect" human that we are. In fact, we weren't designed to be anything other than the human being that we are. We are doing this human being thing perfectly!

The beauty is that we are all evolving toward being more loving and more aligned with the spiritual being that we are, whether we realize that or not. So we can just relax and enjoy the ride that Life is taking us on. All that Life asks is that we choose love over fear and hatred. Fortunately, we all learn that being loving is the only sane choice, since the opposite only leads to suffering. We can't really make a mistake, so nothing needs fixing, because we are all being swept along toward seeing the truth about ourselves and about life—that we are all One and that life is good!

WANTING TO KNOW THE FUTURE

One of the ego's strongest desires is to know the future. It wants to know the future very badly, so badly that it often resorts to making it up, if not in a full-blown fantasy, at least in thoughts and beliefs about the future that constantly change. Sometimes such fantasies are negative and depict the ego's fears about the future. The likelihood of events actually occurring in the often dramatic way the mind imagines is miniscule; and yet our thoughts about the future grab our attention, stir up our emotions, and can even cause us to act in certain ways. The ego creates a problematic future and then takes steps to avoid it. To the mind, thinking about the future seems reasonable, prudent, wise, and practical. But nothing could be more impractical than being detached from the Now and lost in imaginary fears and plans, and actions to avoid those fears.

It's natural that the ego operates like this, because it doesn't trust life. It doesn't recognize the Intelligence behind life, which is wise and loving, and helping us to evolve toward being wiser and more loving. The ego doesn't see that life is good and trustworthy because it's busy telling negative stories about life, about how unfair and unsafe it is. Of course the ego is frightened—it frightens itself with negative stories. It doesn't see the love, goodness, and support that are present, and it doesn't appreciate that challenges and difficulties evolve us in ways like nothing else can. Essence knows the truth about life, but when we are identified with the ego, its beliefs, and the stories it spins, we don't see things as Essence sees them.

We want to know the future because we want confirmation of the ego's belief that the present will be redeemed by something better in the future. We want someone to tell us, "Yes, your prince (princess) will come, and you will live happily ever after." The ego's stance is that whatever is happening isn't good enough, but someday life will be wonderful, and then that bliss will last forever. This fairytale is so deeply embedded in our makeup that we may not even realize we are telling ourselves this story. This belief interferes with experiencing this precious moment. Moreover, it interferes with seeing the truth about life: It is constantly changing, we have little control over it, and it's full of things that are both likeable and unlikeable.

The ego isn't seeing the whole picture when it rejects the Now. It rejects the moment because it focuses on what isn't present that it would like to be present. If the moment isn't providing sufficient pleasure, power, safety, comfort, specialness, superiority, or security, it rejects the moment. But life doesn't exist for the ego's pleasure and to bolster its sense of self. Life exists for all of life, and it contains everything we need to be happy if we are willing to be in the moment without our opinions, beliefs, and judgments.

Stripped of thought, the Now is alive and always changing into something new and unexpected. The Now moves, and it is full of all sorts of things that dazzle the senses, inspire love, and surprise us. The Now is all we need *and* it is all we really have. That the Now can be any other way than the way it is showing up is an illusion. The ego has little power to change what is happening because it's already too late—life has already moved on to the next moment. All the ego can do is interfere, through its dissatisfaction, with having a full and rich experience of the moment. The ego's discontentment saps the joy out of life, so it's no wonder we long for a better moment. The ego spoils the present moment and promises a better one, but a better moment will never come unless the mind becomes quiet or is ignored. And then every moment is good.

When we find ourselves wanting something other than what is showing up right now, it can be helpful to ask ourselves what we think getting what we want will give us. We think we will finally be happy when we get what we want. What we discover when we do get what we want, though, is that even that wonderful moment disappears and is replaced by the next one and the next one. Life keeps moving on, bringing us a mixture of what we like and don't like. Why not like—love—everything that life brings you, because whatever it is won't be here for long, it will never be this way again, and the way it is, is all you've got.

FEAR: THE EGO'S MOST POWERFUL TOOL

Fear is powerful. It can make us do things we don't want to do, and it can cause us to behave badly. Fear is a justification for war and all types of conflict. We are willing to fight and wage war because we are afraid of the consequences if we don't. If we don't fight, we are afraid we won't get what we want, and we are afraid of what not getting what we want will mean. When we feel our survival is at stake, fear is behind that, and that fear is the basis of all wars and other atrocities. Most people will do anything to survive. The questions we need to ask about our fears are: "Is what I'm afraid of real? Is my survival really at stake? Do I know that for sure?" The answers to those questions are rarely yes.

Fears are not real because they are ideas about a future possibility. How real can those ideas be? The future exists only as an idea. Where did that idea come from? This is such an essential question. Fears always come from the ego, because that's what thinks about the future, and how reliable a source is that?

We need to examine not only how real and how true a fear is, but also how functional fear in general is. Do our fears keep us safe or protect us from what we are afraid of? They seem to motivate us to take care of our basic survival needs. For example, we are afraid of being homeless and starving, so we work to earn money to survive. However, if we needed fear to help us survive, then as soon as we had enough money to survive, wouldn't we stop working? So much more than fear is behind our motivation to work and do the things we do. We don't need fear to motivate us to live. We are naturally motivated to live: to work, play, create, rest, explore, grow, learn, have fun, and so on. Essence motivates us to live life. Fear is simply the ego's contribution to life, a contribution we need to examine.

The ego generates fears and tries to get us to do something about them. We believe our fears because we are programmed to believe them. We believe that if we don't do something about our fears, they might come true. Fear is how the ego stays in power because fear gets our attention. It keeps us tied to the egoic mind because the mind promises a solution to the fear. If the ego doesn't have a plan for avoiding what it says we should be afraid of, then it gives us a plan for coping with it: eat, watch TV, drink, do drugs, go shopping. We assume that fear is constructive by motivating us to take care of ourselves, but fear is behind our addictions and self-destructive actions, and it's behind depression and other mental illnesses as well.

The truth is that fear is not constructive. It drives us to do things we don't really need to do and therefore wastes our time. Moreover, fear often keeps us from following our Heart, which is the safest thing we could do. In truth, safety is a false concern, since life has a way of bringing us exactly what we need, regardless of whether or not we recognize that or like what it brings.

We can trust life. Fear is the ego's experience because it doesn't trust life. But the perception that life is untrustworthy is false. Fears are a figment of the ego's imagination. They are generated and upheld entirely by the ego. The ego makes up fears, and because these fears are passed on from person to person and from generation to generation, they seem credible. Since everyone is afraid of the same things, our fears seem worthy of our attention.

As a result, questioning them seems unnatural. Fears are so basic to life, the ego's life, that is. The majority of people are identified with the ego most of the time and, as a result, identified with the ego's perceptions and fears.

Fears keep us out of the Now and in the grips of the ego, which then tries to structure and plan our life for us. Meanwhile, Essence continues to move us and attempts to structure our life according to its intentions. We get to choose what will structure our life. Most people's lives are shaped by both the ego and Essence—their life is a co-creation. Essence works its plan into the life we are creating by following our ego. The situation changes dramatically when we wake up out of the ego because the ego becomes less dominant and Essence becomes more prominent.

Fear scares us into paying attention to the egoic mind. It takes us out of the Now by sounding an alarm, which brings our attention back to our thoughts. A fearful thought is more powerful than other thoughts because of the sense of alarm connected with it. Other thoughts tempt us to go back into the egoic mind, but fearful thoughts scare us into going back to it. The fact that fearful thoughts can produce uncomfortable physical sensations makes them all the more convincing.

If we need to do something to take care of ourselves, like eat better, buy health insurance, or get a job, Essence will inspire us to do that, or it may bring people into our lives who inspire us or help us do that. When Essence uses others as mouthpieces to inspire us, they do it without fear. Those who try to get us to do things by judging or scaring us are acting out of their egos, not Essence.

Essence moves us naturally and joyfully to take care of ourselves, and the only thing that can interfere with that natural movement is our conditioning. The ego is responsible for fears about ill health and also for conditioning that causes us to do things that are detrimental to our health. Our conditioning is what most stands in the way of being willing to work, rest, eat right, and take care of ourselves in other ways. The ego, rather than keeping us safe, as it promises, actually keeps us from our innate wisdom, which knows exactly how to live life safely, healthfully, and joyfully.

DOUBT: THE EGO'S MOST INSIDIOUS TOOL

While fear grabs our attention and yanks us out of the Now, doubt acts more subtly, but has the same effect. While fear is a voice of alarm, even panic, doubt is quite another kind of voice. Doubt sounds reasonable and rational, like sound advice, while actually being infused with fear: "You might get hurt. It's risky. It might not work out." The voice of doubt is a voice we all have heard countless times from parents and others in our lives, who seem to have our best interests in mind but are actually operating out of fear.

Doubt keeps us from following our Heart just as effectively as fear does. Doubt cracks the door open to the unknown negative possibility. It is the "yes but" that takes the wind out of our sails and throws water on our fire. It often takes the form of self-doubt: "I probably won't get that job anyway (so why apply?)." However, more generalized doubt, or distrust in life, can be equally paralyzing: "Nothing I do matters anyway (so why try?)."

A doubt is actually a disguised fear. It is the fear that things won't turn out, that something isn't worth doing, that life isn't good or worth living, or that we aren't good enough. It is belief in the negative. While fear is the belief in a specific negative outcome, doubt is the belief in the *possibility* of a negative outcome. Fear is a doubt that has crystallized into a more specific imagined picture. Doubt is more vague, which makes it more insidious than fear because it's more difficult to refute. With doubt, we aren't sure what might go wrong, but we believe something probably will. And we are probably right! Things probably won't go as planned, and we probably will run into difficulties because that's life. The question is, will that stop you from following your Heart?

Doubts are stoppers. They stop us from doing what we feel moved to do, what our Heart calls us to do. Because doubts come from the ego, not from the Heart, they aren't true warnings that should be heeded. Doubts are the programmed, automatic response of the ego to life: "You better watch out. Life is dangerous. You will fail. You will end up homeless." Our ego and other people's egos spew out the same responses to change or to trying something new. Such doubts are quite predictable. They are programmed into every mind. When faced with the unknown, out come the doubts.

Because doubts come at us from both inside and outside ourselves, they seem believable. If everyone has similar doubts, we assume they must have some validity. We assume there must be something to be concerned about. Fears are contagious; they activate fears in others. The egoic state of consciousness brings out the egoic state of consciousness in others. And all egos agree: The world is a scary and unsafe place. Egos are happy to recount stories of all the terrible things that have happened to them and to others.

Buying into such unspecified fears has kept many people from following their Heart and living the life they were meant to live. Life can be scary, and challenging things happen sometimes. But such things happen whether we follow our Heart or not, so we might as well follow our Heart.

Believing our doubts and fears doesn't protect us from life. We really believe that listening to them will ensure our safety. We also assume that illusionary safety is worth the price of not following our Heart. We are willing to trade the ego's promise of safety, which is a false promise, for the happiness and fulfillment of following our Heart. That's not a very good trade. Life is risky business either way. Why not live it with joy instead of fear and doubt?

THE EGO'S FAVORITE WEAPON

Judgment is the ego's favorite weapon. Judgments are the way the ego protects and fights for its beliefs and the way it establishes its superiority and rightness. Being right and being superior are very important to it, more important than love or anything else. In service to being right and being superior, the ego judges people to bring them down.

When we find ourselves judging others, we feel terrible about ourselves, and then we judge ourselves for that. Although the ego is trying to make itself feel good and superior by judging others, the result is that superiority doesn't feel good. Putting others down doesn't feel good. Separation doesn't feel good—because that's what judging results in. It creates separation, and separation is painful.

Indulging in judgment leads to self-hate, which fuels the need to be superior and be right, so a vicious cycle is born: Feeling bad about ourselves for being unkind and judging can cause us to judge even more in an attempt to feel okay again. There's no way out of this cycle except to see the truth about our judgments.

The ego leads us to believe that our judgments are wise. Judgments are the ego's version of wisdom. The ego believes its judgments are valuable and correct. As a result, they can become cloaked in self-righteousness, which causes people to do a lot of harm in the world. An example is the terrorism that stems from fundamentalism. Terrorists feel justified in any kind of violence, even murder, because they feel that their beliefs are so important to uphold and so right. When judgment is taken to the extreme, violence is often the result.

Love is the opposite of judgment. Love is acceptance. It is accepting our own judgments without acting on them, and accepting other people's judgments and beliefs without reacting to them. The result of acceptance is peace. Therefore, the antidote to war is acceptance. If everyone would let everyone else have their beliefs, it would be possible for people to live in harmony. If people just had beliefs without the judgments that fuel the self-righteousness that leads to fighting, beliefs wouldn't be so dangerous.

We don't realize that judgments are as harmful as they are because, from the level of ego, judgments seem to be valuable and purposeful. However, judgments are very harmful. They damage relationships and undermine cooperation, which is what actually makes it possible for us to survive and thrive in the world. Our survival is enhanced by joining with others, not by fighting with them or trying to gain power over them.

The ego is nasty. When we are identified with the ego, we sound nasty and we feel nasty, and that doesn't feel good at all. When we're aligned with Essence, on the other hand, we don't experience low self-esteem or other negative feelings that come from having judgments about others. There's no such thing as a nasty person, really, only nasty egos. Who we really are isn't unkind, although when we are identified with the ego, we often behave badly. Fortunately, the ego is not who we are.

People want to know how to love themselves. When we are identified with the ego, loving ourselves isn't very easy because the ego isn't very lovable. We come to love ourselves by discovering

who we really are and by experiencing our true nature, which is
love. If all we are experiencing is the ego, then of course, we're not
going to love ourselves.

Loving the Divine within us and within others is easy, once we
are able to experience who we really are and once we realize that
the unkind thoughts, separating beliefs, and judgments belong to
the false self, not to who we really are. Judgments are part of our
programming, which endlessly spits itself out. We had nothing to
do with the programming we were given. We didn't create it. We
didn't put it there. Our conditioning is not a reflection of who we
really are. When we see that, loving ourselves is natural.

HOW JUDGMENTS UNDERMINE RELATIONSHIPS

The ego is in the business of judging. Judging others is how the ego keeps itself separate from others and gains an identity, and how it makes itself superior to others, which helps it feel safe. Judgments are the ego's main strategy for dealing with others. Notice how whenever you are in the presence of others, evaluations and judgments about them and about how you measure up to them become prominent in your thoughts. Judgmental thoughts are normal. Everyone who has an ego (and that's everyone!) experiences the ego marshalling its forces whenever another person comes onto the scene, or whenever we simply think or talk about someone else.

We don't have to get rid of judgments—and we can't—we just have to see judgments for what they are: the ego's automatic response to other people. When we notice the ego reacting like this, we can disengage from those judgments. We can ignore the ego's knee-jerk, judgmental reactions to others and not speak those judgments out loud.

The trouble with judgments is they keep us from love and from connecting with others. They maintain a sense of separation because what we judge is how someone is different from us or different from an idea or ideal we hold. The ego is suspicious of differences, and it separates itself from those who are different—which is everyone! Through judging, the ego rejects those who are different or who don't measure up to its ideas and standards, regardless of whether the ego lives up to these standards itself.

In these times, where we encounter people from all over the world on a daily basis, either in person or through the media, intolerance of differences is a big stumbling block to greater peace in the world and within ourselves. Becoming aware of our instinctual reaction to judge others just because they are different and becoming aware of the negative impact of doing that can bring us a step closer to inner peace and world peace.

In more intimate relationships, judgments eat away at relationships and kill love. Little by little, they poison our relationships, until only anger and resentment are left. We believe our judgments are valid and therefore have a place in our relationships. What we don't see is that they have only enough truth to make us feel we are right, and then the ego uses them to try to manipulate others into complying with our conditioning.

Our judgments are the means by which the ego tries to force others to be what it wants them to be. For example, the judgment "You are so sloppy" is an attempt to get someone to stop being sloppy, according to our definition of "sloppy," which is determined by our conditioning. The ego's strategy is simple: If it can shame others enough, then maybe they will stop doing what they do and start doing what it wants them to do. When we are identified with the ego, we don't realize that sloppiness, or any other label, is subjective. Labels, or judgments, are not the objective truth, but our personal perception, our conditioning. We take our conditioning as the true perspective, rather than seeing that it is only one perspective, while other people have their own perspective, their own conditioning.

We are so convinced that our conditioning is right that we assume we have the right to impose it on others. Unfortunately, they feel the same way about their conditioning. Most conflict in relationships is caused by arguments over whose conditioning is right.

What happens when we have a judgment about someone is we search for proof that supports it. We look for ways that person conforms to our judgment and ignore ways that he or she doesn't. We build a case for our perception and create a story about that person, which interferes with our reacting purely and simply to him or her in the moment. Our ideas and stories interfere with seeing the whole truth about someone, especially how they are right *now*.

Our reactions to someone we are judging are bound to be quite negative, whether we are conscious of those reactions or not. What happens when you feel or react negatively toward someone? Usually, we get a negative response from that person, which reinforces our negative feelings. We often don't realize the part we played in creating that negativity. If you're being judged, or even if you just sense that someone is judging you, how likely is it you will feel positively toward that person and act accordingly? Judgment produces judgment, while love produces love.

In relationships, we rarely see the other person clearly and purely. We bring our projections, beliefs, stories, and histories into the moment, and they cause us to perceive and react to others the way we do. We see how others fit our projections, but not how they don't. We assume things about them that may not be true or are only partly true. We even do this with people we've never met: If they remind us of someone, we respond to them as if they were that person. Or if they trigger feelings in us, we assume they feel a certain way about us. The truth is that others are a mystery to us.

We can't ever really know them. We only think we do. We "see through a glass darkly."

Judgments color our interactions with people, and they produce negativity that dooms relationships to difficulty. The good news is that judgments don't have to matter. They can arise in the mind, as they will, but we don't have to empower them by giving them our attention or giving voice to them. Instead, we can stay in a place of open, innocent, awareness of others, free of our stories, beliefs, opinions, and agenda as much as possible. When we do that, something miraculous happens: love! Amidst the ego's continual flow of judgments and negativity is Essence, which is in awe of the beauty and uniqueness of each moment and of every person. It knows how to meet others with acceptance, curiosity, and love. Fortunately, Essence is who we really are and who the other person is too!

THE EGO IS CONFUSED

Although, much of the time, the ego pretends to know, it is often in a state of confusion caused by disparate voices within itself. The truth is the ego doesn't really know anything. It has no innate wisdom of its own, just information it's gathered from various sources. Although it has accumulated a lot of information, much of it is contradictory and untrue. The ego doesn't know how to evaluate and weigh the information it has, discern what is true from what is false, or apply the information to reality. The ego is a computer and not a sage, although it pretends to be a sage!

The ego pretends to know because that's how it copes with the unpredictability and complexity of life. If it doesn't or can't know something, it often pretends to—and voila! Pretending to know gives the ego a false sense of confidence and security, which, to it, is better than no sense of security. The ego pretends its ideas and beliefs are correct, and if they differ from other people's, it enjoys sparring with them or feeling superior to them. The ego rarely questions its own beliefs. It's quite content to believe what it believes without further examination.

As our ego evolves, which it does, we become more objective about our beliefs and more tolerant of the beliefs of others. Nevertheless, when we are identified with the ego, we hold our beliefs firmly and use them as guides for how to live. Only after awakening do we see that our beliefs are irrelevant and ineffectual programming.

The ego doesn't like confusion. When it is confused, it tries to get out of that state as quickly as possible by making a decision. When a decision needs to be made, confusion usually arises because all the mind has to draw on in making a decision is its storehouse of contradictory information. Other people are often just as confused as our own egos and may also offer confusing and mixed advice. There are nearly as many opinions about something as there are people. And if someone isn't confused, that's no guarantee their advice is good. Confidence in one's beliefs is not an indication of their correctness.

The answer to what to do about something must come from somewhere other than the egoic mind because the ego is not a trustworthy guide. It doesn't know what to do, even though it may pretend to. And other people's minds don't know either, even though they may also pretend to.

There's something else we can draw on for guidance that is clear and unconfused, and that is the Heart. However, the Heart rarely speaks to us through our mind, and it doesn't always reveal the answer when we want it. Following the Heart requires a willingness to live with uncertainty until an answer is received through the intuition. Because the ego is averse to being confused and to not knowing, it often makes a decision before its time for the answer to arise. The ego may change its decision many times, but at least it has taken a stand, which gives it a sense of knowing, at least for a while.

Changing our mind a lot is an indication that we are listening to the ego, because changing its mind is the way the ego copes with confusion and not knowing. When we find ourselves confused, that means we are listening to the egoic mind, which is confused.

Fortunately, there is another option, and that is to find the place within us that is okay with not knowing and that trusts that clarity will arise in its own time. When clarity does arise, it has a distinct feel to it, quite unlike any conclusion the ego might come to. When clarity arises from the Heart, it is accompanied by a wonderful feeling of yes, relaxation, solidity, and certainty. We just know. At some point, the mind might question that sense of knowing or argue with it and make us feel confused again. Ah, the trials of having an egoic mind! Living in the Now requires constant vigilance and awareness of what the egoic mind is up to, while remaining right here in the Now, where even the ego is embraced.

MAKING PEACE WITH LIFE

The ego is at war with life. It is afraid of and angry at life, it doesn't trust life, and it doesn't like life. We feel that way too when we are identified with the false self. Everyone feels this way, at least some of the time, because everyone has an ego, and the ego is similar from one person to the next. Seeing that a fearful, negative view of life is merely the point of view of the ego can free us from seeing life this way.

It's a lie that life is untrustworthy or that it should be different than the way it is. The ego doesn't like life, and feels it is untrustworthy because life doesn't cater to the ego's plans and desires. Of course, life doesn't cater to the ego's plans and desires. It caters to the Whole, not to individual egos. To expect life to do otherwise is to have unreasonable expectations about reality. Every now and then, the ego does get what it wants in life, but life doesn't revolve around our ego's desires.

Once we see the truth about life and about the ego, then it's possible to feel compassion for the part of us that is so unhappy and that has so many unrealistic demands and desires. The ego is like a child because it is a primitive part of ourselves, an irrational and outdated vestige of ourselves that we are outgrowing. We are evolving out of the need for an ego and the challenges it provides in our spiritual evolution. We are waking up out of the ego and discovering what is really alive and living this life, and that is very exciting. Freedom from suffering is possible as we awaken out of the ego and leave it behind. And so much more can be accomplished in life as Essence begins to live more fully through us.

Making peace with life is a matter not only of seeing that the only thing at war with life is the ego, but also of making peace with the ego. Once we realize the ego is the cause of our unhappiness, the tendency is to reject it, to hate it. But peace can't be had when anything, even the ego, is rejected or opposed. Rejection of the ego is a rejection of our humanness. If we reject our own ego, we will reject and oppose other people's egos too, and that only produces more suffering. We need to come to peace with our own ego, our own humanness, so that we can come to peace with other people's egos and the suffering their egos cause. Opposing suffering is just more suffering.

All the evil in the world is caused by people being identified with the unhappy, frightened, angry, and hateful side of themselves, with the false self. We need to understand that the suffering people cause themselves and others comes from this primitive aspect of human nature and is not a reflection of their true nature or their value as a human being. The only thing that allows us to hurt or go to war with others is the belief that they *are* evil rather than that they, like us, are driven by a primitive aspect of themselves that perpetrates evil.

Evil can't be stopped with more violence, which is the ego's response to evil, but by connecting with what is true, real, and good within others. That connection can only be made by what is true, real, and good within us. This may sound hopelessly idealistic, but what choice do we have? The alternative does nothing but perpetuate more suffering and evil on the planet, and we've had enough of that.

Making peace with life requires making peace with other egos so that they can relax and their true self can shine through. When we accept life as it is, we drop into Essence. And when we accept that other people *have* egos, but are not their egos, that helps them experience Essence. The only way out of ego-identification and the suffering it causes is love and acceptance, not opposition and war. This is the transformation that must take place now on the planet.

PART 3

Breaking Free of Conditioning

SEEING THE TRUTH ABOUT DESIRES

Desire is a movement of the ego toward something that isn't here right now. If what we desired were here right now, we wouldn't desire it. If loving what is, is the secret to happiness (and it is), then desiring something that isn't here is the prescription for unhappiness.

Desires always seem reasonable because they are the result of a perceived lack on the part of the ego. It desires something because something about the current experience isn't enough: It's not fun enough, not comfortable enough, not exciting enough, not special enough, not peaceful enough, not easy enough, not fast enough, not loving enough, not pleasurable enough, not sexy enough, and so on. The ego's judgments leave us feeling that something is wrong or missing and that the experience can and should be improved upon. Judgments provide a reason for desiring something, and they create discontentment, which fuels action.

We assume any discontentment we feel is the result of something wrong with or missing in our life. We don't realize our unhappiness comes from taking on the ego's viewpoint. Life just is the way it is, neither good nor bad really. An experience or a situation is the way it is, and that will soon change. Why make it wrong? Nevertheless, dissatisfaction is the ongoing state of the ego, and when we are identified with it, we feel unhappy. Every moment becomes something to complain about, and these complaints fuel actions, many of which are a waste of time and energy, except from the ego's point of view.

Without discontentment, the ego would have nothing to do, no purpose or reason for being. Dissatisfaction fuels activity that supports the ego's goals and values. It motivates us to pursue what the ego wants: more of something or a better something. When the ego gets that, it wants even more or better of that, or it pursues something else.

Desires are forever being generated by the ego. They keep the ego busy and keep us tied to its goals and agenda. If we buy into the ego's desires, our life will be structured accordingly. Few realize their desires are the cause of their unhappiness rather than the cure and that they don't have to pursue them.

Desires, like all thoughts, arise out of nowhere. Where do they come from? Why do you want one thing and not another? Desires are somewhat individual, since each of us is unique, but all egos want generally the same things: power, security, pleasure, safety, specialness, superiority, attention, praise, success, money, and possessions. Our specific desires are influenced by what those around us want and what we've enjoyed in the past: If we've liked driving a BMW, we might want a BMW. We often want more or better of the things we have positive associations with. That's natural. We're programmed to want more and better of everything.

The problem with wanting more and better of the things the ego wants is that having more and better of these things doesn't necessarily result in happiness. In fact, more and better of some things can actually be a problem. We can have too many cookies, too many love affairs, too many possessions, and too many activities. Even when that is the case, the ego often still wants more and better. It doesn't know when to stop pursuing what it has decided it wants.

We get caught up in our desires because they seem like more than just thoughts. Desires are very convincing. The thought "I want" seems important, true, real, and compelling. We feel motivated to do something about it, if only to put an end to the uncomfortable state of desiring.

Not having something we want feels uncomfortable, like life is lacking something, but also like *we* are lacking something, and we won't be happy until we get it. Feelings of lack come with every desire. They are packaged with the thought "I want." If this thought didn't have such feelings attached to it, ignoring our desires would be much easier.

Most people don't want to detach from their desires. They love their desires. They enjoy desiring, or so they think. And they can't imagine life without their desires, nor do they want to. They haven't realized that their desires are the cause of their suffering. Until they do, they will continue to pursue them. Detaching from our desires is impossible without seeing that desires are not the route to happiness that we assume they are. So are you convinced that desires are the cause of suffering and that there is another way to live besides going after what the ego wants?

Desires take us out of the Now, where it is possible to be content with life as it is. The ego doesn't want contentment (it needs discontentment to exist), so it turns away from the Now as soon as it experiences contentment, which it considers boring and uninteresting. The ego wants its fantasies and the drama that comes with trying to fulfill them. We want this drama too, until we don't anymore. At a certain point in our evolution, we become tired of the ego-driven drama, and we long for the peace and contentment that only our divine nature can provide. That peace and contentment are available only in the Now, not in some moment in the past or future, but in *this* moment right now.

When we are finally tired of pursuing the ego's desires, we are ready to see what is really going on. What we find is that the ego's desires are trumped up and made up. They have little relevance to our life and little wisdom to guide our life. In fact, pursuing them often wastes our time and energy while yielding scant fulfillment. All this ego-driven activity and the dissatisfaction that results is meant to point us Home, back to the Now, where something else is alive and moving us according to its intentions.

Essence's intentions are felt deep within us as drives, longings, urges, and inspiration. They don't appear in our mind as the thought "I want," although at some point we are likely to put them into words. These deeper desires don't mislead us or take us away from fulfillment, but bring us closer to it. They are the desires we are meant to follow. However, if we are caught up in the ego's ideas and goals, we might not notice these more meaningful drives.

As we evolve, the difference between the ego's desires and Essence's drives becomes increasingly clear, and ignoring Essence's callings becomes more difficult. Following Essence results in joy and a feeling of being true to ourselves. That joy feels very different from the stress and unhappiness we feel when we are being pushed by the tyrannical ego to get more of something or something better.

Detaching from the ego's desires isn't difficult once we see their falseness and become aware of the deeper, more meaningful desires driving us. How is Essence moving you now, in this moment? The answer to that will give you a clue to what Essence's intentions are for you. We discover these intentions, not by looking in our mind, but by noticing what is coming out of the moment. Thoughts of "I want" might be showing up, but what else is here in the moment? What is here that is more true and real than any thought?

FEELINGS ARE NOT WHAT YOU THINK THEY ARE

Feelings, like desires, are not good guides to life. They don't have the answer for what to do, either in the present moment or in our life in general. And yet for most of us, feelings drive actions and structure our lives to a large extent. When we have an emotion, we often feel compelled to act it out or say or do something in response to it. We often say or do things we wouldn't have if we hadn't had that feeling. When we are experiencing an emotion, that feeling feels important, real, and true—and like a problem we need to solve.

Most actions that stem from emotions are an attempt to fix or do away with the unpleasant feeling. They are an attempt at a solution to the unpleasant feeling: "I'm bored, so I'm going shopping." "I'm angry at my boss, so I'm going to quit my job." "I'm lonely, so I'm going to have an affair." "I'm sad, so I'm going to eat this pint of ice cream." "I'm unhappy, so I'm going to steal this." "I'm frustrated, so I'm going to blame you." "I'm miserable, so I'm going to make you feel miserable." Feelings result in a lot of useless and destructive activity that squanders the present moment.

If such "solutions" to our feelings worked and were good ones, these actions would make sense. However, many reactions to our feelings are vindictive, unkind, destructive, ill-conceived, and unjustified. They are vindictive and unkind because they come from the ego, which is vindictive and unkind. They are destructive (including self-destructive), ill-conceived, and unjustified because the ego lacks wisdom and insight.

Emotions are based on conclusions, mostly erroneous ones, on the part of the ego: We believed, expected, or desired something, and someone or life didn't comply with that. So we feel angry, sad, betrayed, and so on. The error was in believing that life *should* conform to our beliefs, expectations, and desires, when most of the time it doesn't. Who says that life should conform to our wishes? The ego, of course, which continually argues with reality. This disagreement with reality is the source of unhappiness, not circumstances.

When we are in the grips of the ego, we react to our negative feelings in a number of ways: We may act them out in destructive or hurtful ways; we may blame, judge, or belittle others; or we may act self-destructively. Such reactions spread negativity and consume a great deal of our energy. And in the end, they don't get us what we really want. They don't reap love, appreciation, or respect, but discord and more negative feelings, although we may feel better temporarily or briefly enjoy feeling self-righteous. So much energy and time is spent absorbed in negative feelings and unnecessary, ill-informed activity and drama, while we could have had a very different experience.

The unfortunate results of reacting to our feelings seem obvious enough when we aren't having any emotions. But when we are in the grips of our feelings, we don't see very clearly. Feelings put us in an altered state of consciousness of sorts. They take us over and turn us into irrational creatures who are willing to do nearly anything in the moment to be right or get our way. Emotions are not only a poor guide for what to do, but a destructive force. If someone told you to tell someone off, quit your job, be belligerent, eat a whole cake, or cry and scream until you get your way, you probably wouldn't listen to them. But if our feelings or mind tells us to do these things, we just might.

We are programmed to identify with our emotions, to believe they are important and meaningful, and to act on them. We aren't taught that there's another way to relate to them besides repressing, suppressing, or expressing them. The other way to deal with our feelings is to just notice and accept them but not act on them. Once we know how to relate to them, then having feelings becomes easier. They stop being such a problem.

Emotions are part of our conditioning and a product of the ego. They don't come from Essence. Emotions come from thoughts, or the particular conditioning we have, which are for the most part poor guides for our behavior. If you observe your thoughts closely, you will see that they are mostly negative and designed to uphold the beliefs, opinions, and identities that the false, or conditioned, self holds so dear, many of which don't deserve upholding. These negative beliefs, opinions, and narrow identities separate us from others and make us feel disconnected from life and our very own life force, the same life force that is coursing through and animating every one of us.

We listen to our mind and follow our feelings because we think there's nothing else to listen to or guide us. The ego doesn't notice that something else is and always has been guiding us, which is Essence. The ego's ignorance or denial of what is real doesn't change the facts, however: We are the life force that is living through us and not the ego, which attempts to control our life. When we drop out of the mind and into the moment, even briefly, we know the truth about ourselves. Then it is possible to experience Essence's guidance and wisdom.

Essence doesn't produce emotions, but it is experienced as positive feelings: joy, elation, peace, contentment, acceptance, love, patience, wisdom, and compassion. Essence steers us toward its intentions with these positive feelings and away from what isn't compatible with our life plan with a sense of "no" or with feelings of sadness. Essence's guidance rarely shows up as words in the mind, but when it does, those words ring true, and we feel expansive and joyful, which is quite different from how most thoughts make us feel.

Most thoughts are negative. They disparage us, life, or others, and they represent reality too narrowly. Most thoughts are a small story told about a moment in time that can't begin to contain the whole truth for us or anyone else. Our thoughts are the spin that our conditioning puts on reality. Many of them create negative feelings that cause us problems and hurt others.

For example, even a simple thought like, "I'm blocked," can make us feel sad and affect our outlook for a day or even longer. Once we feel sad, the ego tries to justify that feeling by building a case for it. The ego creates a story around the sadness: "I'm sad" becomes "I'm sad because I'm blocked. Nothing ever turns out right for me. Everything I try fails. I can't get anywhere. What's the use of doing anything? Nothing I do matters." The more attention we give our feelings and this flow of thoughts, the more the story grows. And as the story grows, our feelings grow. Now we really do have a problem. Now our feelings are interfering with getting things done, being happy, and our relationships. How can we be present to life and others when we are absorbed in our own story of failure and sadness?

What a terrible waste of time and energy it is to tell such sad and incomplete stories. But that's what the egoic mind is designed to do. It tells tales, we believe them, and we respond with feelings and actions. That becomes our experience of life, while a much more pleasant and peaceful experience is possible. When we stop listening to the mind, we stop producing negative feelings, and we discover that we have so much more energy for life and the real experience that is available in the moment.

Fortunately, the stories the egoic mind tells are not the whole story about life, which is potentially much more joyous than the ego's experience of it. Once we stop listening to the mind's version of life, we can begin to experience life as it really is, and we discover that life is good! Behind all of life is Goodness (God-ness), and you are that!

FEELINGS DON'T TELL THE TRUTH

When we have a feeling, such as a feeling that things are going wrong, a feeling of being lost, or even a feeling that everything is going well, it isn't the truth. Such feelings come from stories we tell ourselves about whatever we're experiencing or about what is going on. We weave the events of our life into a story, that story causes us to feel a certain way, and those feelings make our story seem true! You think: "If I feel this bad, things must not be great. If things were great, I'd feel a lot differently." But the truth is you feel the way you do only because you believed your own story.

For instance, when things seem to be going wrong (as they often do in life), we might take those difficulties personally and tell a sad story, such as, "Things never go right for me" or "No matter how hard I try, nothing works out" or "I must be doing something wrong." The ego has a tendency to personalize events. It turns them into a story that relates back to the *me*. However, the truth about any event or string of events is much bigger than can be contained in such a small, personal story. Things just go badly sometimes, and when they do, it means nothing about you or your life. And when things go well, it means nothing about you or your life.

It's funny how we can suffer over a story. We can suffer over a story as much as over an event. In fact, events don't cause suffering; our interpretation of events, our personalization of them, causes suffering. The negative feelings that result from the story we tell ourselves reinforce the story, like a feedback loop: You tell a story, the story makes you feel bad, and those feelings convince you that your story is true. So you continue to tell that story, which continues the loop. We get stuck in these loops, which have very little to do with reality. When others are caught in one of these loops, we are often able to see how they are creating their experience, but when we are caught in a loop, seeing this is not as easy. Except there is one big clue: our feelings!

Negative feelings are a sign that we have a story going about an event in our life. If we weren't personalizing it, turning it into a story about *me*, we wouldn't have feelings. Feelings don't come from events at all. Even when something devastating is happening, there isn't time for feelings. The crisis happens, and afterwards the feelings come. Feelings happen after events, not during them, because feelings come from recalling events and telling a sad, personal story about them.

Feelings are caused by the memory of an event plus a personalization of it: "This happened to me, and it shouldn't have happened." Feelings become part of our present experience, but they are created by entering the ego's reality, a memory of the past, and fabricating a story about that memory. Then before we know it, we are feeling something. That feeling, which is happening in the present, is real and feels real, although it isn't based on anything real. Feelings are convincing because they are a real experience in the present moment, even though they aren't based on anything but a story.

We waste so much time and energy creating feelings without realizing we are doing it or how pointless it is. We create needless pain for ourselves and others by doing this. Events are what they are, and when they are over, they are over. If we don't bring events from the past into the present through memory, we can simply experience whatever is happening now. In the simplicity of the moment, are peace and contentment.

Once we become more aware of the stories the ego is spinning, we can become free of the feelings and suffering caused by these stories. Feelings don't tell the truth about life; they only reflect the ego's truth—its story. Not only can we live without that story, but we can live much, much better.

FEELINGS POINT TO CONDITIONING

Feelings can be an ally in our spiritual growth rather than a destructive force. Unpleasant feelings point to conditioning–ideas, beliefs, opinions, judgments, desires–that is false. The proof that such conditioning is false is that it results in negative feelings, and negativity is anti-life, anti-love. Any idea you have that results in a negative feeling is false. That idea is not the whole story, but a partial truth, and partial truths are lies.

Any negative feeling you have, then, can be used to uncover mistaken beliefs and misunderstandings that belong to your conditioning. Most of the time, our beliefs go unrecognized and unchallenged. We generally assume our thoughts are true: "I think it, so it must be true!" We are programmed to believe what we think. The suffering that is caused by our thoughts and the feelings that stem from them eventually gets us to question our thoughts.

Suffering is ultimately what gets us to stop going down the same road. That road just becomes too painful to keep traveling, and we begin to look for a way out of our suffering. Fortunately, there have always been people who knew the secret to happiness. The Oneness doesn't leave us without resources to overcome our suffering and difficulties. When we are ready to find our way out, we discover those resources.

The way out of suffering is actually through our feelings. By being very present to our feelings when they are occurring, we can discover how our beliefs created them. In that discovery, lies our freedom. Once we realize that our beliefs are the cause of our feelings, we can become free from having feelings, or at least from being tossed to and fro by them.

However, we all have a lot of beliefs to see through. Behind every feeling are a number of ideas you've been believing, or you wouldn't have that feeling. You have to uncover these beliefs and see for yourself that they are false. For every belief you uncover, ask, "Is that true?" The answer is always no because no belief is completely true.

Every belief has some truth to it, just enough to get us to buy into it. However, what underlies feelings are not facts, but stories, perspectives, perceptions, points of view. These stories are subjective, not objective. If they aren't working for you (and they aren't if they are making you feel bad), then change them or ignore them. They don't have to be your stories. They aren't yours.

Your true story is Essence's story. What would a loving, wise parent tell you? That is what Essence would say. The truth is that love is at the core of the universe, even in this dimension where there is so much suffering. All of our experiences are not to punish us, but to evolve us and bring us Home. Besides, you created them and designed them for yourself.

You can tell a sad story about life if you like, but it won't be the truth. Life allows us to feel sad for as long as we want. But eventually we discover that there is another possibility, and that is to embrace life as it is, with all its messiness and difficulties, and to love life for the experience it is providing us. We love our experience just because that is what's happening and because the alternative—to hate it, to be angry, to be sad, or to reject it—is just not an acceptable alternative. We don't have to suffer if we make the right choice.

WHAT TO DO WITH FEELINGS

When we are feeling something, the tendency is to express it in some way, either emotionally by crying or yelling, physically by kicking or hitting, or verbally by talking about it. These expressions of feelings are not constructive, although talking about our feelings in a therapeutic setting can be. What most people verbalize when they're in the grips of an emotion only feeds the emotion and can be destructive to themselves and their relationships. When emotions do the talking, what comes out isn't pretty!

Letting our emotions do the talking is very different from psychotherapy, where an emotional experience is talked about after the fact in an environment where insight and a more rational perspective can be brought to it. Looking back at an emotional experience can be helpful, especially when the goal is to uncover the mistaken beliefs and conclusions that caused and fueled the emotion.

The same objectivity and inquiry can be brought to an emotion while it's being experienced, instead of allowing the feeling to be expressed in whatever way we are used to expressing it. Without something intervening to stop them, emotions tend to be expressed automatically, unconsciously, and repetitively. They are like storms that sweep over us, and for the duration, anything goes. All stops and inhibitions are gone. Many people say things when they are upset that they deeply regret. Nevertheless, when the storm hits again, the same unconscious responses repeat themselves.

The answer to dealing with an uncomfortable emotion doesn't lie in going to another room and pounding a pillow, although doing that is better than pounding a person or something else. Pounding a pillow won't result in any insight into the emotion or any healing or evolving of that emotion. When feelings get triggered, it's an opportunity to discover something about our conditioning and heal it, and expressing the emotion or pounding a pillow won't facilitate that healing process.

A more productive way of working with emotions than expressing them, acting them out, or pounding a pillow is inquiring into the cause of an emotion while we are experiencing it. By doing that, we are taking responsibility for creating the emotion, rather than blaming someone else for it. Taking responsibility for our feelings allows for the possibility of discovering what is behind a particular feeling. When we take the time to examine our feelings, the likelihood that we will create those same feelings again is lessened. This is how emotions can be evolved and emotional patterns broken.

Uncovering the cause of an emotion doesn't involve examining external causes—what someone said or did to us—but internal causes—what we said to ourselves to create that emotion. All emotions are instigated by thoughts, which are part of our conditioning. When something happens, certain thoughts come up, and those thoughts shape our experience of that event. We see our experience a certain way because of how we *think* about it. And how we see an experience determines how we feel about it and react to it.

We are so used to blaming others and circumstances for how we feel. Our language even reflects this: "You hurt me." "That made me so angry." Most people don't realize that circumstances don't cause feelings. Rather, the story we tell ourselves about an experience or a circumstance causes us to feel a certain way. When we change the story we are telling about something, then our experience of it changes. And our reactions and responses to it are likely to change as well.

The ego is so quick to blame others for how it feels. And yet the ego is the sole creator of feelings. That's an interesting setup. The problem is that most people haven't acquired the objectivity needed to step back from their feelings and inquire into them instead of react to them. Even those who are able to be objective about their feelings might not know enough to inquire into them, since that usually isn't part of our emotional education. We are only now beginning to see what is actually so obvious: Thoughts create emotions. If we change or disregard our thoughts, feelings aren't created.

The way to deal with feelings when you are experiencing them is to let them be there and find out what thoughts are behind them. What did you just say to yourself that caused you to feel that way? Is that how you *want* to feel? If not, then don't buy into those thoughts. It's really that simple. If your thoughts aren't serving you, disregard them. Put your attention on something else.

Being objective about our emotions is only possible if we have gained some distance from the ego and had some experience with Essence. Those who are deeply identified with the ego will find stepping back from their feelings very difficult to do. But the alternative is quite unpleasant. Having feelings is exhausting, unproductive, and damaging to us physically and to our relationships. Negative emotions sap our energy, waste our time, and cause us to be ineffective. When we are in the grips of them, we can't think or act clearly, we make bad decisions, and we function poorly. There are many good reasons for mastering your emotions.

When an emotion is present, instead of doing what you would usually do, just be with it, with a gentle and curious attitude. Look to see what story you just told yourself and believed. The story is usually something like, "This shouldn't have happened. This is unfair. This is terrible. I can't stand this." All this raging against life doesn't help us cope with the situation. Believing such thoughts and expressing them just creates feelings that make us less capable of handling whatever is going on. The ego feels justified in having such feelings, and it justifies them with more thoughts, but do you really want to go down that road?

You don't have to. There's another possibility, and that is to realize that you don't have to have unpleasant feelings. Life is lived perfectly well without all those negative emotions. If you don't identify with the thoughts that create those feelings, you won't experience those feelings. And if feelings do arise, they don't have to take you over when you see they are based on the ego's narrow and negative perspective. The ego's perspective doesn't have to be yours, and you don't have to give voice to it.

You have the power to choose how you see your experiences and your situation, what story you tell about them. Eventually we all learn to tell wiser, more positive stories, the kind Essence would tell, if it told stories. Once we learn to ignore the mind's stories, we discover that life can be lived in harmony and with very few negative emotions regardless of what happens.

HEALING EMOTIONAL ISSUES

Emotional issues aren't healed by acting out or giving voice to our feelings. Doing so only strengthens the conditioned beliefs behind the feelings and reinforces our tendency to react to emotions this way. When we react emotionally to events, whether the reaction is anger, sadness, belligerence, hopelessness, blame, guilt, shame, or whatever, that response becomes part of our emotional repertoire. If that response is repeated enough, moving into that emotion becomes automatic, unconscious, and compelling.

We all have certain emotional reactions that have become habitual. They have become so familiar that we may feel like we don't have a choice in how we react, even though we always do. Emotions take us over, and we are lost in them for a while. Examples of emotional patterns might be flying off the handle whenever we don't get our way, contracting into feelings of worthlessness whenever someone criticizes us, or moving into self-pity whenever something goes wrong.

The first step in turning an emotional pattern around is becoming conscious of the reactive pattern when it's happening. The second step is accessing the will to behave differently. The third step is bringing awareness to the emotion. Healing an emotional pattern requires not reacting to a feeling in the usual ways and not repressing it either, but just being with it, befriending it, allowing it to be there, and bringing awareness to the energetic experience of it.

Being with an emotion this way is very different from identifying with it. Rather than experiencing ourselves as angry, sad, or whatever, we experience the energy of the emotion as a curious observer, as if we were outside of the emotion. Being able to be aware of an emotion places us outside of it. We are noticing the emotion rather than responding unconsciously to it. We are experiencing the emotion from the perspective of Essence rather than being identified with it.

Bringing awareness to anything allows us to know it in a way we haven't known it before. When we are identified with an emotion, we aren't aware of it, but just reacting to it. Being identified with an emotion and bringing awareness to it are two very different things. Identification with an emotion reinforces it, and bringing awareness to it heals it.

When we bring awareness to an emotion, we can discover where the emotion came from and how the beliefs behind it don't serve us. For instance, you might realize that whenever you overwork, you feel angry. Behind the anger, you discover this story: "No one ever takes care of me (and someone should). So I have to work hard to take care of myself, or I might not survive." With further inquiry, you realize that you came to this conclusion as a child because you didn't feel taken care of.

Once you discover this story, you can decide whether you will keep telling it to yourself and whether you can forgive your parents for not giving you the support you needed as a child. When you realize that holding onto this story and not forgiving what happened long ago doesn't serve you, then you can let go of that story. When you do that, working hard will cease to make you angry. You realize that this story caused you to overwork, when you didn't need to overwork. You might begin treating yourself more kindly, as you would like to have been treated as a child, and treating others more kindly becomes easier too. You end up feeling better about yourself, others, and life, all because you are no longer driven by the mistaken conclusion you came to as a child.

Such insights can set us free from the conditioned self and all the pain that comes from believing false stories. Emotional wounds from our childhood and the conclusions we drew as a result of those wounds shape our perceptions about ourselves, others, life, and God. If we never see the falseness of these conclusions, they can interfere with our functioning or make us depressed. Inquiring into our feelings exposes these conclusions and frees us from them. Seeing the truth does indeed set us free. Inquiring into our feelings takes a little faith, willingness, and persistence, but what's the alternative? Once we realize there's a way out of the suffering caused by our emotions, we can hardly go back to them.

DISENGAGING FROM THE EGO'S VOICE

For most people, the ego's voice is a constant companion, although often not a welcome one. The egoic mind is nearly always talking to us about something: It scolds us, judges us (and others), scares us, pushes us, parents us, explains things to us, gives us information, tells us what to believe, tells us what is right and wrong, reminds us to do things, tells us how to do things, evaluates what we do, conjectures about our future, ruminates about the past, and befriends us.

The ego is usually a negative voice, but it can also sound positive: It builds us up, congratulates us, and imagines fantastic possibilities for us. However, this puffing up is generally followed by a tearing down at some point. The ego's positive comments take us out of the Now and away from Essence just as much as its negative comments do. The ego tells us we are terrible or wonderful, and both are lies. Whatever stories it tells are incomplete and simplistic.

In every moment, the ego tells us who we are, according to its beliefs and assessments: "You are stupid. "You are brilliant." "You are no good." "You are special." "You will never be somebody." "You will be famous." Such evaluations create a self-image, which mediates between us and the world and interferes with experiencing reality as it is showing up in the moment.

The ego's negative and positive comments grab us. We really think it has something important to say, and we listen with great curiosity. We value the ego's opinion—until we don't any longer.

When we are identified with the ego, we believe what it believes so much that we are willing to fight, even kill, over our beliefs. Identification with the ego is the root of all evil in the world and the cause of all suffering. The egoic mind has nothing to offer us. But it takes a real commitment to discovering this before we are free of the ego. We have to see through the ego again and again before it stops having power over us.

What makes the ego especially tricky is that it changes guises frequently: When we are onto it as a complainer and refuse to listen to its complaints, it may pretend to be kind and wise, in the hope that we will listen to its advice. If we stop listening to it when it tears us down, it may try to get us to listen to it by complimenting us. It will even pretend to be our spiritual mentor and try to mentor others by mimicking a wise tone of voice and repeating wisdom it's heard. When we finally see that the ego has nothing of value to say, it tries to be our buddy and hold conversations with us like a best friend. The ego is tricky, but once we know its tricks, it can't fool us any longer.

The truth is the egoic mind has nothing of value for us, not even as a friend or companion. If we continue to hold friendly conversations with it in our head, we will continue to live in our head rather than in the Now, where communications from Essence are received. Holding chats with the egoic mind may seem harmless, but it strengthens the mind and alienates us from life and from Essence, which needs our cooperation to unfold our life according to its plan and intentions.

Chatting with the mind passes the time, like chatting with any friend, but being involved with it in this way won't bring fulfillment or lead to happiness. This friend is not a wise friend, and conversing with it is a waste of time and energy. Once we really see that, we can begin living from a deeper and richer place, a place where joy, contentment, and peace are possible.

ONE THOUGHT AT A TIME

There is only room for one thought to arise at a time. People often feel overwhelmed by their negative thoughts and feel victimized and controlled by them. They have difficulty detaching from them. They feel that their thoughts, at least some of them, are too compelling to ignore, and some *are* very compelling.

Nevertheless, many of our thoughts are quite easy to ignore, and ignoring the easier ones strengthens our ability to ignore the ones that are harder to ignore. Learning to detach from the mind is a skill. Like every skill, starting with something easier and then moving to something more difficult is the way to build confidence and competence. The most important thing is to not get discouraged and give up trying to detach from the egoic mind, because the ego will try to discourage us when we attempt to free ourselves from it.

Once you see you can detach from, or ignore, some of your thoughts, it will be easier for you to believe you can detach from all of your thoughts, even the ones that have negative feelings tied to them. When you are learning this, please be gentle with yourself. Ignoring the mind isn't easy. We have paid attention to it and believed it for the most part all our lives, so the mind has been reinforced nearly constantly. Besides, we are programmed to pay attention to and believe the mind, and that programming isn't easy to overcome. As a result, breaking the habit of listening to the mind can be a slow process, and there's nothing wrong with it taking some time.

Whatever efforts you make to detach from the mind matter. Every time you successfully ignore a negative or irrelevant thought, which is most thoughts, it becomes easier. Irrelevant or unnecessary thoughts are much easier to ignore than negative ones because negative thoughts are entangled with our identity. Irrelevant or unnecessary thoughts are any thoughts that don't serve our functioning in the moment.

Notice how often your egoic mind just chatters about irrelevant things, including the past and future. You can easily see that you don't need thoughts about the past and future to function in the moment. So to start with, try ignoring all of those thoughts. Doing that will also get you used to noticing what your mind is up to. You will discover how unnecessary or negative most of what you think is. This can be very enlightening! Most people don't evaluate what they're thinking because they're so absorbed in their thoughts. Once you learn to observe your thoughts, you are well on your way to becoming free of the egoic mind, its negativity, and the suffering it causes.

Once you are more aware of your thoughts, you can evaluate them. You can ask, "Is that true?" What is able to be aware of and evaluate your thoughts is Essence. One way Essence liberates us from the tyranny of the egoic mind is through our capacity to notice and evaluate our thoughts, which is a capacity of Essence. Ignoring our thoughts becomes a lot easier once we learn to notice them and once we see how untrue, irrelevant, and negative they are. If your thoughts are untrue, irrelevant, and negative, why would you give them your attention? Seeing how false and unhelpful our thoughts are naturally frees us from them.

Nevertheless, some thoughts are deeply connected to our identity and laden with emotions. They are thoughts we identify with and believe automatically and unquestioningly. We may not even be aware that these thoughts are affecting us. These are the most difficult ones to ignore because they seem true. We believe them, and we may have believed them most of our life. Thoughts that have fear or other negative feelings attached to them seem particularly real and true, even though they aren't. If we are willing to examine them through inquiry, by asking, "Is that true?" we can discover that even they are false.

Any thoughts that have produced negative feelings need to be unmasked. We need to ask, "What did I just say to myself that created that feeling?" The negative beliefs behind the feeling need to be uncovered and seen as false. Freedom may not come easily, but it is so worth it. Besides, the alternative, entrapment in the ego, is just not acceptable.

A RADICAL INQUIRY

Here is a question that can have a radical impact on your life if you use it for serious inquiry: "What are the lies I am telling myself?" This question can uncover the ways we pretend to know something when we don't, for example: "I'll be doing this the rest of my life." "She'll never change." "I'll never fall in love again." This question can also uncover the many negative stories we tell that aren't completely true, for example: "I can't do anything right." "No one cares about me." "She always treats me that way." "I can't trust anyone." "Nothing ever turns out for me." This question can also help us realize how often we may argue with something that already happened, for example: "He shouldn't have done that." "Life shouldn't be so hard." "I shouldn't have slipped up like that." Statements with *shoulds* in them are lies because they pretend that the past could have been different than it was.

To summarize, there are three kinds of lies we may be telling ourselves:

1. Pretending to know something when we don't. When you catch yourself pretending to know something, ask, "Do I really know that's true?" You may be surprised to discover how often you pretend to know something. It is the ego that is pretending to know because knowing, even pretending to know, makes the ego feel safe.

2. Negative stories. When you catch yourself telling a negative story, notice the contraction and tension that telling that story causes and decide you don't want to do that to yourself. Decide that negativity isn't acceptable to you anymore. Why would you want to believe stories that make you feel bad? Why would you punish yourself that way? Such stories come from the ego and give it a sense of identity and a problem to solve, which gives the ego life.

3. The big lie: "Life should conform to my desires." When you catch yourself indulging in a *should*, simply see the truth that the purpose of life and our particular life's purpose is not to fulfill our ego's desires. The purpose of life and our life's purpose are much bigger than our ego's desires.

At first, it might be difficult to see that our thoughts are lies. They can be very convincing, and we are used to believing them. Even if our thoughts make us feel bad, we may cling to them because they are familiar and therefore somewhat comfortable. They give us a sense of identity (e.g., "I'm not okay") and the only sense of identity we have if we aren't familiar with our true identity as Essence (goodness). There is another identity awaiting everyone's discovery, and that is our true identity.

The way you know you are aligned with Essence rather than the ego is that you feel good. You don't feel contracted and tense, but accepting, at ease with life, expanded, and open. Instead of saying no to life, like the ego does, Essence is the experience of saying yes to life. Everyone knows what saying yes to life feels like.

Truly, the only thing in the way of experiencing the peace and ease of Essence is believing the ego's lies, the seemingly harmless and seemingly true thoughts that constantly float through our minds, which appear to be our thoughts. But these thoughts aren't ours; they belong to the false self. They don't reflect Essence's experience of life. When we are able to break through the spell cast by these thoughts and the sense of limited self spun by them, we experience the truth, and the truth is good!

When you feel good, you are aligned with your true nature, and when you feel bad you aren't. What a wonderful Homing device we have built into us! Try giving up all the thoughts that make you feel bad, or even just some of them, and see how doing that changes your life. You don't need negative thoughts. All they have ever given you was a false self that suffers. They are all lies.

ACCEPTING DEATH AND LOSS

Death and loss are some of the most difficult things we experience
as humans. We become attached to the way things are and
therefore resist change. We become comfortable with life being a
certain way. In part, we just love the sameness, the predictability,
the familiarity of having things the way they've been. We like
sameness so much that we may even feel sad when a situation we
haven't liked ends, just because we were used to it.

Much of our resistance to death and loss is a resistance to the
unknown, even a fear of it. We like the known, even when that
situation isn't that great, at least we know what to expect, or we
think we do. The unknown is scary because we project our fears
onto it. Not knowing what's ahead feels like stepping off a cliff,
and we imagine the worst. Much of the suffering around death and
loss is caused by our fear of an unknown future, our fear of what
will happen next. But the truth is that we've never known what's
going to happen, and even now we don't know. That fact is
glaringly apparent when we lose something that was part of our
familiar world.

What we fail to see when we lose something is that something
else is taking its place. Birth and death are always happening, even
moment to moment: The present moment is already turning into
the next moment, and the new moment isn't the same as the old
one. Something new always takes the place of something that has
gone. The problem is we usually don't know what that will be.
What is being born often takes a while to show up. Or, in the

midst of our grief, we may not be aware of what has already been born.

During times of loss, a belief that life is good and a willingness to accept loss as a part of life is very helpful, since the mind tells us the opposite—that death and loss are bad and shouldn't happen. The mind paints negative scenarios of the future without the loved person, animal, or object. It imagines that we will never get over the loss and we will never be happy again. The egoic mind turns something that is very natural, death and loss, into a disaster.

Death and loss are natural. They are a reality of life that we have to accept. To rail against what is natural makes no sense. To be angry at life for allowing death and loss is like being angry at the sky for being blue. Birth happens and death happens. Seeing and accepting that both are true and part of life is so important. Birth brings new life into this dimension, and death takes something whose time has come away. What will happen next is anyone's guess. It may be a birth or a death, but both are happening equally. When we see the whole truth about life—that death and birth happen in equal measure—then death becomes easier to accept.

The mind makes death difficult to accept by telling us lies: "This shouldn't have happened. You will never be happy again. This is too painful to bear. Life is cruel." Those are very sad and untrue stories, and we will suffer if we tell ourselves such stories. We can just as easily tell a story about death and loss that is true: "It must have been time for this to happen. Life goes on. I will find a way to be happy again. Life is a blessing, and I will treasure it all the more because of this."

What makes it difficult to see that the egoic mind is the cause of our suffering is that most people are caught up in the same negative mind. So our own negativity is supported by other people and gets reinforced by them. If you're not suffering over something that other people would suffer over, they might assume you didn't love whomever or whatever you lost. Some grieving is meant to demonstrate our love for another, unconscious as that may be. But such grief is unnecessary. Loved ones who have died don't benefit from our suffering. In fact, those who have crossed over often tell their loved ones to stop grieving and be happy for them because they exist and are doing well in another dimension. Grief and sadness don't serve us or anyone else.

Of course you may miss what is no longer here. When you are feeling that way, notice what is having the experience of missing. The *I* is. The missing is showing up in your thoughts as, "I miss...." How are you creating the experience of missing? Missing is a feeling, so you must be saying something to yourself, consciously or unconsciously, that is causing you to feel that way.

We don't have to experience missing something or someone. One reason we create and perpetuate the feeling of missing is because it's a way of honoring and expressing love for what is lost. Under the guise of love, the ego draws us into suffering. Does missing have anything to do with love? When you explore the feeling of missing, you discover that it is created by idealized images of the past and future. Do these images serve you? Do they make you happy or sad? You can be sad as long as you like, but sadness is unnecessary. Missing is just the ego's way of keeping us tied to the past and to itself.

We can move through a loss gracefully or with great suffering. Finding a way to do it gracefully is our spiritual work. Losing something or someone we love provides so much opportunity for spiritual growth. We can wallow in our pain, as our ego would have us do, or we can find another way to be. The other way is to be involved in the here and now, not in our thoughts about the past. Life is coming out of the Now, and something new is always showing up. Pay attention to what is being born now. The past is just a memory, and we will never get any satisfaction from a memory because it's just a thought. Why bring a memory into this fresh new moment? It doesn't serve. You can choose peace and happiness over suffering—if you want.

LETTING GO IS LETTING GO OF A THOUGHT

Letting go seems so difficult at times, but whatever we are trying to let go of is already gone. It's in the past, and life has moved on and is bringing something else. All that is ever really left to let go of are our thoughts about something in the past. Letting go naturally happens when we are just here right now, in the moment. The Now is free of the past, unless we bring the past into the Now through thought.

Thought is the only thing that can disturb the peace and contentment of the Now. Even a shocking event is here only briefly and then gone. The only way a terrible event lives on is through thoughts about it. We may be dealing with the effects of such an event for a while, but the loss itself is over. Every moment provides plenty of resources for dealing with the effects of a loss, and those resources will be much more accessible if we aren't caught up in negative thoughts and feelings about the past.

We can't control what thoughts come up in our mind, and when there has been a loss, thoughts about that loss are bound to come up. However, we can control how much time we spend with these thoughts. The difference between heaven and hell is largely a matter of how much time we spend dwelling on thoughts about the past.

We dwell on such thoughts because we think it serves us in some way. Through thought, we try to fix or rewrite the past ("If only..."), we create a story about the past to defend or punish ourselves, or we analyze the past to try to prevent certain events from happening again. But none of these strategies changes the past or helps us cope with what happened. They are the ego's strategies, which are designed to make it look good, make others look bad, keep it safe, or justify its existence. But the ego's goals aren't worthwhile or a good use of our energy. Thoughts about the past that attempt to fix it or keep it alive just aren't useful, and they keep us from noticing what life is bringing us in the present moment.

Life gives and it takes away in equal measure. The cycle of birth and death is natural and not wrong, as the ego assumes. What passes is meant to pass. It's gone, and the situation can't be different. Nothing can change the past, including thought. However, dwelling on thoughts about the past does change our experience of the present moment. When we drag the past into the present, everything else that belongs to the Now is marginalized and overlooked. All we see is the past or, more accurately, our story about it.

All we can ever have of the past is our story about it, and that story is very unsatisfying. Our stories about the past don't feed our soul like the Now does. And worse, any story is usually a sad tale that keeps us caught up in negative feelings, and then those feelings become our experience of life.

These negative feelings are so unnecessary. When we turn our attention to what is here right now and away from the past, negative feelings can't be maintained. They disappear. No one can maintain negative feelings indefinitely. No matter how depressed, angry, or hurt we are, we eventually drop into Essence and stop feeling those feelings. Having negative feelings is exhausting. Often through sheer exhaustion, we drop into Essence and find relief from our feelings.

Letting go is difficult because that seems to require letting go of what we love. But letting go isn't about letting go of our love for whomever or whatever we've lost. Love is eternal, and our love continues. Our love is what we have left of what we have lost. Letting go of the person, experience, or thing has actually already happened because he, she, or it is already gone. There was no other choice or possibility but to let go. All that is actually left to let go of is our *desire* for the situation to be different.

Letting go of the desire for things to be different is not so difficult when we see that life simply can't be different than it is. Seeing the truth renders the desire for things to be different useless. All we have to let go of is our belief that things can or should be different than they are. They can't. Accepting this makes letting go of the desire for things to be different possible. Letting go naturally follows from allowing life to be the way it is, from accepting that life is as it is. Acceptance is actually the only sane choice because to do otherwise is to create tremendous suffering for ourselves and others, which life allows us to do, of course. But that suffering serves no one.

The good news is that the desire for life to be different than it is, is just a thought. No matter how powerful a desire may seem to be, desire is just a thought, and thoughts can be ignored. We are much more powerful than any thought or desire. We have the power to choose to feed a desire with more thoughts, which results in feelings, or to turn our attention to something else, to what is going on in the Now. Turning our attention to anything other than the desire for things to be different transforms our experience of the moment. Suffering disappears.

The Now has everything we need to be happy if we don't bring any demands into it for it to be different. Doing that isn't necessarily easy, but suffering isn't easy either. Thank heavens there is a choice, a way out of suffering. This is proof that goodness is behind all life and that life is leading us toward greater peace, love, and happiness, no matter what happens.

SURRENDER

Surrender is really just acceptance: We surrender to, or accept, the way things are, the way life is showing up. Surrender and acceptance seem so difficult to the ego. That's because the ego doesn't want to accept life, and that will never change. We will never get the ego to surrender to life, to go with the flow. Resistance is its natural state. When we are identified with the ego, we feel the ego's resistance. However, when we are not identified with it, but in touch with who we really are, accepting life just happens.

During your day, you have many experiences of being surrendered to life as it is. You may not notice those moments because you move through them so smoothly and peacefully. The moments of resistance are the ones we tend to notice because they make us feel like we have a problem. We are taken farther out of the Now as we try to fix the problem we think we have or try to feel better, for example, by eating, fantasizing, shopping, or watching TV.

Escapist activities are activities that help us become unconscious of our feelings, including the feeling of resistance to life. We often cope with feelings and other aspects of life we are resisting by avoiding the experience we are having and doing something that will distract us from what we are resisting and, hopefully, give us some pleasure. We often try to relieve the pain of resisting life with pleasure. Seeking pleasure is one way the ego copes with life. The irony is that the ego is what creates the resistance to life and therefore the suffering—not life. The ego's solution to its own resistance is to seek pleasure. When we are identified with the ego, we are involved in this cycle of trying to avoid pain and seeking pleasure.

Surrender is the way out of this cycle. When we surrender to life as it is, we experience a simple joy and fullness that's much more satisfying than any pleasure we could experience. The simple joy of just being is complete enough. Nothing needs to be added or subtracted. The moment just flows into the next, without the need to change or fix anything about it.

Surrender allows us to experience life as it is unfolding instead of experiencing our resistance to it. When we are identified with the ego, we aren't experiencing life, but our resistance to it. We are actually missing the experience of the Now because we're not in the Now, but involved in our thoughts about whatever is going on or about something else, and that's a very different experience.

Our thoughts about whatever is happening are never like being in the Now, even when they are pleasant. Thoughts are just part of what is happening in any moment, and if we ignore nearly everything but our thoughts, we will have a very narrow and dry experience of life. Life can't be replaced by thoughts about it. The only way to experience life is to say yes to it, to surrender to what is going on right now and really experience it rather than think about it. Saying no to what is happening entangles us in the mind's story about and resistance to what is happening, and we suffer.

The way out of suffering is to notice the ego's resistance to life and ignore it. Every time that resistance appears, notice it and then bring yourself back to what you are experiencing right here and now: how your body feels, what you are sensing, what you are moved to do, and what intuitions are arising. Just stay here in the Now. What you discover when you stay in the Now long enough is that the Now feels good and is rich and ever-changing. From the Now, life isn't experienced as a problem. The egoic mind is the only thing that makes life into a problem.

Once you realize you can relegate the egoic mind to the background and just enjoy the moment, you will choose to do that more and more. Surrendering to life isn't hard at all. It happens simply and naturally whenever we stop paying attention to our mind's version of life and start paying attention to life itself as it is coming out of the Now. There's something else to do besides think! And that is to notice, to be aware of what is happening now. Notice, look, feel, listen, sense, and give yourself fully to the experience you are having, and you will drop into the Now.

LIVING WITHOUT MIRRORS

How we look is so important in this culture. How we look becomes how we see ourselves. The image in the mirror seems like who we are. We carry that image around with us inside our heads, and when we think of *me*, we think of that image. We have many self-images, and our inner image of what we look like is perhaps the strongest. We are most identified with that self-image because identification with the body is so strong and because the mind needs something to pin the idea of *me* on.

Our inner picture of ourselves strengthens and holds in place the idea of *me*. Without that inner image, the idea of *me* weakens and can't be maintained as easily. You may have experienced this when you were away from mirrors for a while, like when you were camping or in a more primitive living situation. You begin to experience yourself more as you really are than as an image you hold in your mind of yourself.

There's a big difference between the experience of ourselves and the experience of an image of ourselves. The image is an idea. An image of ourselves is flat, un-alive, and we have to work hard to maintain it (especially without mirrors to help us), while the experience of ourselves is mysterious and ever-present. The experience of who we really are is just there. We don't have to work at producing it; we just have to notice it.

Who we really are is experienced as what is looking out of our eyes. This is very mysterious: What is it that is looking out of your eyes? Take a moment and notice what it's like to look out of your eyes and experience yourself that way. What a different experience it is from imagining what you look like in your mind's eye.

When we experience ourselves looking out of our eyes, we experience our body very differently than when we imagine our body or when we see it in a mirror. Stop a moment and just look at the miracle that is your body, without any comments or thoughts about it. What do you experience? You are likely to experience the body as something apart from yourself, something you look upon with amazement. Whose hand is that? Whose leg is that? The body appears to be more of a vehicle for who you are than who you are. And so it is. The body is a vehicle for who we really are. The mind pretends that vehicle *is* who we are, but the body is only a temporary carrier for the consciousness that is looking out of our eyes.

Through the formation of an inner image, the mind takes us away from the reality that we are not the body. That inner image is made possible by mirrors and other reflective surfaces. Without them, we wouldn't know what our body looked like. We would experience ourselves without having an inner image of ourselves. The mind would still form other self-images, perhaps a made-up image based on how people react to us. Identifying with an image of ourselves would be much harder if an image of ourselves wasn't constantly being reinforced by mirrors.

To begin to live more from the real experience of ourselves rather than from an image of ourselves, we don't have to get rid of mirrors, although living without them for a while can be helpful. We can just realize we are not the body and consciously choose to put our attention on what is looking out of our eyes rather than on what we think other people see when they look at us.

Noticing what is looking out of our eyes results in a dramatically different experience of ourselves, and it allows us to be much more present to life. Maintaining a self-image is hard work, and it interferes with being present to whatever else is going on. When we give our attention to our self-images and thoughts, we miss so much else that is going on. The ego overlooks and discounts much of what is happening and assumes nothing is happening. It tries to draw us out of the moment and into thinking. It doesn't give life a chance to reveal its richness. When we give our full attention to life instead of to our thoughts, we discover the happiness and contentment we've always wanted but haven't been able to find in the ego's world. Ideas just can't substitute for real life.

LIVING WITHOUT REFERRING TO BELIEFS

Beliefs, like self-images, are ideas that end up shaping our reality—if we believe them. Everyone has more beliefs than they are aware of, since many beliefs are unconscious. We acquired our beliefs from experiences in this lifetime, and even from other lifetimes. We acquired them from what we've read and what others have told us and taught us. We are constantly refining and reformulating our beliefs, and these beliefs matter—if we believe them.

Living without referring to our beliefs is unimaginable to most people. And yet the awakened life is one that doesn't look to beliefs for how to be in the world or for what to do. We actually don't need our (the ego's) beliefs to live life. Being awake is a place of being very present to what is coming out of the flow, or the Now, and responding to that without thinking about it. Living like this sounds dangerous to the egoic mind—doing something without thinking about it first, imagine that! And yet, we do this all the time. Many times throughout our day, we feel moved to say or do something, and we act spontaneously on that.

Being awake means being awake in the Now, being aware and alert to what is arising to do and say in the moment. There is such wisdom flowing through the real you. It knows exactly how to be and what to do in any moment. We don't need our beliefs to evaluate what is coming out of the flow or tell us how to live our life. When we turn to our beliefs for how to live our life, they only confuse us. That's because we hold so many contradictory ones.

There is no formula for living life, although beliefs pretend to be. They are what the ego draws on for guidance. But the ego's beliefs are not good guides. The ego doesn't know what will make us really happy or what our life, or life in general, is all about. The ego pulls out a belief and slaps it on reality: "It's raining, so I better go inside now." What if you didn't follow that formula? Essence might want to play in the rain. Who knows? We don't know anything until we do.

The ego makes decisions about what to do based on what we or others have done in the past, not on what is arising in the moment to do or not do. The ego compares each moment to similar ones in the past and responds according to what it concluded about that time in the past. The ego uses the past as a template for responding to the present, but the results of the past aren't sufficient to inform our actions in the present. Moreover, following a formula for how to act takes the joy out of life.

No moment is the same as another. The ego doesn't like that, so it ignores that fact. It brings its template and agenda to the moment and reacts accordingly. It doesn't respond to the moment purely, but through its own lens of beliefs and self-interest. Its overarching question is, "Am I getting what I want now?" The answer is often no. What the ego wants is highly colored by its beliefs. For instance, if it believes that happiness lies in being comfortable, it will desire comfort, and that desire or some other desire is likely to shape how it responds to the moment. The ego may be focused on comfort or the lack of it and not notice other things that are happening.

The ego has very specific beliefs and, consequently, very specific desires for every moment, which the moment rarely delivers. As a result, the ego goes about trying to modify what is happening to fit its desires. Seeking after a better experience can keep us very busy. When we are doing that, we are not only failing to noticing what's coming out of the flow, but also being kept out of the flow by being so busy planning for a better moment.

This is the state most people find themselves in. Living by referring to our beliefs is a dry and uninteresting place. It's no wonder the ego wants more of something or something better! Living in the mind is a deadening and un-alive place. To liven things up, the ego seeks more things, better experiences, more excitement, more fun, and more pleasure than whatever is here right now. From time to time, the fun and excitement the ego wants do show up. Until they do, the ego looks to its fantasies and plans for the future to fulfill itself, which are inherently unfulfilling. The ego causes the experience of the moment to be dry and dull, and then it tries to correct that flatness with fantasies and actions that attempt to fulfill those fantasies.

Being in the Now and living life from there is an experience of living without beliefs, because we realize that beliefs are unnecessary and only take us out of the Now. When we begin spending more time in the Now, we don't want to leave it. Once we see the truth about beliefs, they lose their power to lure us out of the Now. We realize they are just thoughts that come and go and that they are not *our* beliefs.

WHAT ARE YOU BRINGING INTO THE NOW?

The only thing that exists is the present moment, the Now, but we, as human beings, have a particular relationship with our thoughts that takes us out of the experience of the moment. Thoughts create an alternate reality, a subplot to the Now. We get lost in that pretend subplot and don't notice other things about the moment. When we bring that alternate reality into the moment, our experience of the Now changes. It colors the Now. We are no longer experiencing the moment purely, but through the lens of the ego, which generates our thoughts and feelings.

Our thoughts and feelings come and go in the Now. But unlike sights, sounds, and the other things that come and go in the Now, thoughts and feelings change our experience of the Now when we identify with them. Nothing else that comes and goes in the Now has the same effect on our experience of the moment. The Now is just what it is, but our *experience* of it changes if we are identified with thoughts or feelings. If we aren't identified with a thought or a feeling, we will feel the peace of the Now. If we are identified with a thought or a feeling, we will feel anxious, restless, discontent, and possibly some other negative feelings.

When we think about the past, we bring a memory of it into the Now and then experience our memory's version of the past instead of experiencing the Now. We do this most often with disturbing events from the past, and that reanimates the unpleasant experience and obscures the peace and contentment of the moment. Even a happy memory can take us out of the peace and contentment of the present moment and cause us to suffer because thinking about a happy moment from the past often makes us long for the actual experience that that memory isn't able to produce.

Whenever we identify with our thoughts—any thought—we lose touch with the peace and contentment of the Now. We often think that whatever is happening is making us unhappy, but what we're bringing into the peaceful moment through thought is what is making us unhappy. Once you realize the result of bringing thoughts into the Now, you can choose to not give your attention to your thoughts. Notice how you immediately relax when you give your attention to what is present right here and now instead of to your thoughts and feelings.

We think we need our thoughts and feelings to function. We think they make us who we are. But we don't need thoughts and feelings to function, and they aren't who we are. They belong to the false self that we *think* of ourselves as, but they aren't what is alive in us, living life and experiencing the present moment. What is experiencing the present moment, including what is aware of contraction caused by identification with thought, is who we are.

What is experiencing the present moment is very silent, unlike the egoic mind that chatters constantly. Who we really are is the silent Experiencer who is alive and having the experience that the false self is creating. We can wake up from the false self and begin creating more consciously from Essence, from the Experiencer. We don't need the false self to experience life. It has never been what has been experiencing life, but what has kept us from experiencing life joyfully.

STAYING IN ESSENCE IN AN EGO-DRIVEN WORLD

Staying in Essence in an ego-driven world isn't easy. Being around egos can pull us into our ego. Being in the world means not only being around egos, but also being around advertising, television, and other media that reinforce the ego's values: "Be beautiful, be rich, be powerful, be sexy, be young," the media tell us. The media tell us such things, not just once a day but many times throughout our day, through pictures and words.

Pictures are a particularly powerful medium for conditioning us. They go straight through any filters we have to the unconscious and program it. Even though we may not like or approve of the message we are receiving from the media, that message is still affecting us. Conditioning continues to happen every day. It isn't something that only happened when we were young.

Pictures, and television in particular, are an especially powerful means for programming children because, unlike adults who may turn off the television or ignore advertising, children sit in front of the television and take in what they're seeing. Children aren't discriminating enough to know what isn't true and what isn't good for them. Like a sponge, children absorb whatever is presented to them.

Adults and children are being programmed in damaging ways today by the media. We are being programmed to want things we don't need and eat things that aren't good for us. And worst of all, we are seeing violence regularly, which sends the message that violence is a normal way to deal with life, that it is an acceptable response to difficulties. To think that violent images don't affect children, teenagers, and adults is to ignore the evidence around us and the prevalence of violence in our culture and even among children, which doesn't naturally occur. Children naturally hit each other, but they don't kill each other, and today, even that is happening.

To expect that we can stay in Essence when we are being bombarded by the ego's values from the media, other people's egos, and the stress produced by an ego-driven lifestyle is expecting too much. So what can you do? When you want Essence more than anything else, you create a lifestyle that supports Essence, one that gives it room to flourish. It would be a lifestyle that has much less stress and busy-ness, much less striving, and a somewhat slower pace. The world needs this anyway. It doesn't need more people racing around after everything the ego wants. Consumerism is what has gotten us in trouble environmentally. In looking for happiness in things, we are destroying the environment and wasting our natural resources.

Consuming will never make us happy. That is obvious now. Today, more than ever, we need to choose more consciously what we spend our money and energy on. When we give our energy and attention to getting what the ego wants, we perpetuate an ego-driven lifestyle. But when we give our energy and attention to what is real and capable of providing true happiness (e.g., connections, creativity, learning, growth, service, peace, and love), we discover that we don't need so many things, and we finally have time to just be, which is what we've always wanted anyway.

If, one by one, we begin to create a lifestyle that supports Essence, the tone of our society can turn and become more peaceful, humane, and nourishing in the deepest way. Much of the consumption in our culture is an attempt to fill a hole that can never be filled, a hole that is the ego, which is never satisfied. All the while, true nourishment is available right here in this simple moment.

A LIFESTYLE FOR AWAKENING

The lifestyle of most Americans isn't conducive to awakening, either to becoming awake or staying awake. It's designed to attain the ego's goals: money, power, status, comfort, pleasure, beauty, possessions, and security. Our American culture gives lip service to other values, such as love, kindness, and togetherness, but the ego's values come first.

In our culture, we see what the ego wants as necessary. We don't think we will survive or be happy unless we achieve a certain level of power, comfort, security, and material wellbeing. The sense of needing such things is very deeply ingrained in us, so much so that we don't question our devotion to these goals. If we do question these values, we run into opposition and fears from others, who sincerely believe we won't be happy or survive without putting the ego's values first.

Fortunately, there are plenty of examples to the contrary, of people who have put their Heart's, or Essence's, desires above the ego's, and who are happy, fulfilled, and surviving well. We assume we have to choose between the ego's goals and following our Heart. However, these two things are not necessarily mutually exclusive. Following our Heart can result in getting what the ego wants. Even when it doesn't, the fulfillment that results from following our Heart is more than enough, and the material things we might have had won't seem important.

Because our culture is so focused on having fun and acquiring things, people are very busy working, playing sports, going places, and shopping. Their lives are a whirlwind of activity, with hardly a moment to just stop and see what's going on, on deeper levels, or just experience the fullness of the Now. People take much pride in how hard they work, how busy they are, and how little they rest. In a culture driven by the ego, there's little time for contemplation, meditation, walks in the woods (what woods?), creating, gazing at the sky, playing with children, or just being.

The spare time people do have is often spent in front of the television, watching other people's harried and problem-driven lives. Advertising and most television programs reinforce the values of our culture and the ego. Watching television makes us want to be richer, more beautiful, more powerful, and more successful than we already are, and it often causes us to be dissatisfied with our lives. Television convinces us that happiness lies in the ego's superficial values.

Everywhere we turn, we are confronted with the ego's values and with people who are struggling and striving to look better, be better, and get more and better things. To awaken from the egoic nightmare, we first have to see that the world the ego creates is a nightmare. Then we have to be willing to make other choices, to structure our lives in a way that puts what matters most to us first.

What does matter most to you? What do you really want? This is a very important question. It's fine if what matters to you is getting what the ego wants. Sometime, in this lifetime or in another, that will change. Just be clear that awakening isn't a way—a more spiritual way—of getting what the ego wants. Awakening is the realization that what the ego wants is irrelevant to life and to our happiness. What does Essence want? That is the question. What is the deepest desire of your soul for this lifetime and for this moment? If your deepest desire is to awaken, you will feel that, and you will be drawn to work, activities, people, and a lifestyle that will support that.

People often make the mistake of assuming that being spiritual or being awake means they should be able to do any kind of work and be in any kind of living situation and still be happy, no matter how unsuitable or stressful that situation might be. While it's possible to be happy in every moment, certain kinds of work and living situations suit us better than others. When we are awake, we naturally involve ourselves in situations that fit Essence's intentions for us and avoid situations that don't. If we don't do that, staying aligned with Essence and being happy will be a challenge.

Being involved with work, activities, and acquaintances that aren't aligned with Essence's intentions for us and don't support being awake—being in the Now and living from the Now—will make awakening more difficult. This may seem obvious. However, people often want to awaken because they feel stuck and unhappy in the life they have created, and they assume awakening will make it possible for them to be happy in those circumstances without having to change anything. But awakening is more likely to move us out of unsuitable circumstances than allow us to remain in them.

If your life is already aligned with Essence's intentions, it will be infinitely easier to awaken, especially if you make time to meditate, rest, and just be. Meditation, resting, and just being are important before and after awakening because these activities help us become aligned and stay aligned with Essence. To discover what Essence intends for us, we have to be in the Now. A life full of stress and involvement with the egoic mind takes us out of the Now and out of touch with Essence. Essence can still reach us, but if we are dedicated to the ego's world, will we listen?

Essence requires some stillness daily and a willingness to listen and be guided by Essence rather than by the ego. The ego will try to keep us tied to it with fears—of not being rich or beautiful or powerful enough, of not having enough, of not being loved, and so on. The egoic mind tells us that following our Heart is dangerous and that we won't survive or be happy if we don't listen to the mind. Disregarding such fears takes courage and trust. So what will you trust—the ego or Essence? Which is more trustworthy? What are you trusting now, if not Essence?

PART 4

Secrets to Happiness

HAPPINESS IS HERE RIGHT NOW

Many people would define a successful life as a happy one, so we go about trying to be happy in many ways. Some people try to attain happiness through accomplishments and material things, while others use spiritual means. The problem is that happiness isn't something to attain or achieve, but something to notice. If you are busy trying to achieve happiness, you are probably overlooking it. The ego tries to get happiness from doing, having, or being someone, while the spiritual ego tries to get it from transcending all of that. For the ego, spiritual freedom, or enlightenment, is just another thing to be achieved.

Wanting happiness and freedom from the suffering of the ego are worthwhile desires. The problem is that wanting anything implies you don't already have it. You *believe* you aren't free when you already are. You *believe* you need to do something to be happy, and you don't. That truth is very hard for the ego to grasp. The ego doesn't notice the happiness that is already present in the moment because that happiness doesn't look like the ego imagines or wants it to look.

When true happiness shows up, the ego is bored with it: It's too plain, too ordinary, and it doesn't leave us feeling special or above the fray. It doesn't take away our problems, which is the ego's idea of happiness. The ego wants no more difficulties: no more sickness, no more need for money, no more work, no more bad feelings, only unending pleasure and bliss. Such perfection is the ego's idea of a successful life. However, the happiness the ego dreams of will never be attained by anyone. The ego denies the reality of this dimension, where challenges are necessary to evolution and where blissful states and pleasures come and go.

The happiness that underlies all of life is happiness that comes from just existing. Happiness is actually a quality of our true nature, of Essence, which loves challenges because Essence loves the growth that comes from them. It embraces all of life, not only the pleasurable and fun moments, but also the more difficult ones.

Then who is life difficult for? The only thing that experiences life as difficult is the ego, which is made up of ideas about ourselves and ideas the conditioned self has about life. These ideas are all that interfere with true happiness. Ideas—just thoughts—keep us from experiencing life and the happiness that Essence is experiencing as it is living through us.

In any moment, you can experience true happiness if you just notice that true happiness is here right now. True happiness is much more subtle than the giddy high we feel when we finally get what we want, which never lasts for long. The ego wants happiness to feel like a high that never goes away, which is also why many people want enlightenment. They imagine enlightenment will be a state of unending bliss, which it's not. In short, the ego wants every moment to be thrilling. But life will never feel that way. No one has ever had the experience of unending excitement or bliss in this dimension, and no one ever will.

True happiness—the happiness that *is* available and ongoing in this dimension—is a quiet contentment with life and an openness and availability to life. True happiness is steady and constant, although it seems to come and go as our attention shifts. Usually our thoughts take us away from the happy peacefulness of the moment because the ego doesn't appreciate peace and prefers drama and feelings.

If we stay in the Now long enough, we experience Essence rejoicing in life, relishing the experience of being alive in this ever-changing and mysterious moment. That contentment and love of life is true happiness. It doesn't have the excitement or glamour of a spiritual experience or winning the lottery. But unlike those thrilling experiences, true happiness doesn't come and go.

When we are aware of everything that is arising in the moment, not just our thoughts, we see that life is unfolding perfectly, regardless of the ego's attempts to manipulate it. The ego tries to intervene in every moment, as if it's responsible for shaping life. But the ego is not that powerful. The ego's interventions take us away from life and bring us into its mental world, where it creates an imaginary life full of dreams, hopes, and fantasies—the life it wants.

The life the ego wants will never come to pass, however. What the ego wants is unrealistic and often not connected to the flow of life, out of which reality is born. Life doesn't follow the ego's desires. Life has its own momentum and reason, which is mysterious and can't be known ahead of time. The ego doesn't like not knowing and not being in control, so it pretends that it can be the creator of life, and through the mind it is. But the mental world the ego creates doesn't affect life except by taking us away from it.

The ego's mental world is an illusion that will never become real. The ego really believes in its illusions, though. It believes its dreams and fantasies may come true if it thinks the right thoughts and does the right things. The ego doesn't recognize that something else is at work, giving birth to life. When we are in touch with what is actually creating life instead of the ego's ideas about life, we stand a chance of being really happy, not because of anything that happens, but just because we exist in this miraculously ever-shifting moment in time and because what we are loves life.

The Now is complete and fulfilling just as it is. Nothing needs to be added to it. The Now can't be made any better because the Now is already as good as it gets. The ego will tell you otherwise and promise you its version of happiness, but the ego's promises are empty. Will you chase after the ego's dreams, or are you willing to see that happiness—true, unshakable happiness—is already here and that what is here is enough?

BEING SATISFIED

The ego looks around and says, "Okay, there's this. Now, what else?" The ego doesn't notice what is here, only what *isn't* here. It overlooks the potential for enjoying what *is* here and, instead, imagines the enjoyment it might have in the future over something else. It fantasizes about better things and better experiences, because that is how the ego is designed. It's designed to be future-oriented and goal-oriented. It isn't designed to appreciate the way things are.

It's a good thing that who we really are does appreciate life just as it is, or there would be little chance for happiness. The happiness we do experience comes from our true self, Essence, which is in love with life. We also experience brief bursts of happiness when we get what we want, but that kind of happiness never lasts because the ego soon wants more or wants something different. It's never satisfied for long.

Essence is always satisfied because there's always plenty to be satisfied with. The sky is blue, gravity keeps us on the planet, experiencing is happening, and every moment is new and different. Essence loves experience for experience's sake. It loves to see what will happen next. When the ego isn't getting what it wants, it complains, "Nothing's happening. I'm bored." "Nothing's happening" is the ego's story, and that story is never true. Something is always happening. What you are seeing now is different than what you saw just a moment ago. What you are hearing now is different than what you heard just a moment ago.

What you will have for lunch is probably anybody's guess. We don't even know that much about life.

The ego pretends to know what's going to happen, and pretending to know makes it feel bored with life. But the ego doesn't ever really know. It doesn't like to not know, however, so it pretends to know. When we allow ourselves to not know, life becomes much more interesting. Then we can experience the excitement, curiosity, and love that Essence feels toward life. But when we believe the ego's tale of woe—"Life is boring. I'm bored. Nothing's happening. I need something else"—then boredom becomes our experience.

When we approach the present moment as the mystery that it is, life becomes juicy and interesting. We don't know what will happen next, and we never will know the future. That's the truth. The mysteriousness of life makes life fun. The ego takes the fun out of life by demanding that life be a certain way and declaring that it doesn't like life the way it is. Taking the ego's point of view makes us feel we need something more to be happy than what we already have right here and now.

The great lie is that we need anything to be happy. The happiness, or joy, of Essence as it is experiencing life through us is available right now. Essence loves everything about the present moment and the next moment, no matter what is showing up. It loves how the chair that is holding you up feels. It loves the experience that is coming in through your senses. It loves the feeling of the breath coming into and leaving your body. It loves the miracle that is your body. It loves that the universe works, that it all holds together and supports life. It loves that people are kind to and support each other. It loves that people learn from their mistakes. It loves that evil eventually evolves into good. Essence loves it all. Life is such a gift. We don't need more of anything to experience life as a gift, and that's the greatest gift of all! What goodness and Intelligence there must be behind life for life to be able to provide all that it provides. Life is a miracle and a blessing.

ALL YOU HAVE IS NOW

The Now is the only reality. It's all that really exists. The past is a memory, the future is a fantasy, and memories and fantasies are just ideas, and quite inaccurate ones at that. Thoughts arise in the Now, but they are only a small part of it. However, because we are programmed to pay attention to the egoic mind, thoughts often take the place of experience: We *think* about life and *think* about what we are experiencing rather than experiencing life purely, without thought. Experience colored by thought and experience uncolored by thought are very different experiences.

When we are identified with the ego, we enjoy thinking about life more than we enjoy experiencing it. The ego doesn't like pure experience because it is left out of pure experience. So the egoic mind tries to convince us that it has something to contribute to the present moment. What it tries to contribute is advice about how to live our lives. But the ego isn't wise enough to guide us, not only because it is made up of conditioning, which is an inadequate guide for living *now*, but also because the ego and its values and goals (e.g., superiority, more, and better) are not worthy ones and therefore can't lead to true happiness and fulfillment.

Fortunately, something much wiser than the ego is already guiding us—Essence. But Essence rarely uses the mind to do that. Essence guides us through inspiration, intuition, urges, motivation, and spontaneous actions. We don't need the mind as much as we think we do. We only need it for functional purposes. We don't need the egoic mind at all. That aspect of the mind is archaic, outmoded. You discover just how unnecessary the egoic mind is when you stop listening to it and start listening more to your intuitions and the spontaneous urges and inspirations of Essence as they are revealed in each moment.

When we are in the moment without giving our full attention to our thoughts, as we usually do, we discover that many things are part of the Now besides thoughts. The ego discounts these other things, seeing them as unimportant and uninteresting. If we pay attention to the ego, we won't have a chance to find out about these other things for ourselves. When we finally become disillusioned with the egoic mind's complaints, judgments, poor guidance, and version of reality, we begin to look outside the mind for true happiness and wiser guidance.

The problem with the egoic mind is not only that it gives poor advice, but also that it keeps us from realizing the wisdom that is available from Essence. Essence allows us to follow the egoic mind, while Essence guides us as much as we allow it to. Once we become more aware that Essence is actively at work in our life, we can begin to cooperate with it more, and life can unfold much more smoothly.

There are a number of things in every moment that we might become aware of, and they change very quickly. Rather than nothing going on, which is what the ego thinks, a lot is going on in every moment. In any moment, we may experience:

1. Input from our senses, including energetic sensations, bodily sensations, sights, sounds, smells, and tastes;

2. Emotions arising from the ego, including anger, disgust, frustration, sadness, happiness, fear, shame, jealousy, envy, guilt, hatred, greed, lust, and excitement;

3. Thoughts, including desires, memories, fantasies, judgments, complaints, opinions, beliefs, doubts, hopes, wishes, planning, observations, stories, rehearsals for the future, ruminations about the past, and other ideas and conditioning;

4. Communications arising from Essence, including intuitions, psychic impressions, inspiration, insights, ideas, creativity, knowing, clarity, wisdom, motivation, and urges to act and speak; and

5. Feeling states arising from Essence, including love, peace, joy, awe, bliss, acceptance, elation, gratitude, happiness, and contentment.

In every moment, many of these things are happening all at once, so there's a lot to give our attention to. Paying attention to communications and feelings from Essence is most important because they are meant to guide our life. Paying attention to sensations is also important because they keep us in our body and out of our head. When we find ourselves identified with the egoic mind, paying attention to sensations brings us back into the Now and into alignment with Essence.

On the other hand, paying attention to thoughts and the emotions that result from them takes us out of Essence and into ego-identification if we believe those thoughts and emotions. Without thoughts, the only "feelings" that would arise would come from Essence: love, joy, elation, happiness, contentment, gratitude, acceptance, awe, and peace. These aren't emotions, but more like positive feeling states.

In any moment, our attention is moving around: It may go from a thought to a feeling, to a bodily sensation, to an intuition, to a sight, to a sound, to another bodily sensation, to another thought, to a sensation of the energy body, to an upwelling of awe, to peace, to contentment, and then to another thought. Every moment is unique in the experience it offers, and every moment is constantly changing into the next.

We don't have control over what arises in any moment, but we can control where our attention goes, and that determines our experience. Any moment can be an experience of peace and contentment or one of upset and dissatisfaction, depending on where we put our attention. If we put it on thoughts and emotions and identify with them, we won't experience peace and contentment. But if we put it on our sensory experience or the positive feelings, intuitions, urges, and inspiration that arise from Essence, we will be content and happy. Attention is the secret to happiness!

GOOD ENOUGH

For the ego, nothing is good enough, and if we take on its attitude, we will never be happy. To counteract this mental voice that is rarely content and always pushing for more and better, the mantra "good enough!" can be very useful. That phrase can neutralize the negative effect of the ego's belief that something isn't good enough. Notice how you can just relax when your attitude is "good enough" rather than "not good enough."

The mind will tell you this is a dangerous conclusion because you won't be successful—*you* won't be good enough if you settle for something being good enough. If we didn't feel that whatever was not good enough didn't reflect badly on us, on our self-image, then something not being good enough wouldn't matter so much.

We decide something isn't good enough (good enough for whom?) and then try to make it better. Who something isn't good enough for is the *me*, who we think of ourselves as. Isn't it interesting that a self-image can have that much power? Our self-image drives us to behave in certain ways.

We are driven by the ego to uphold our idea of ourselves as more perfect than we perhaps are. After all, we aren't very perfect, are we? No one is, but we fight this reality by working very hard at being better than we've been in the past or better than someone else. We set unrealistic standards, and when we fail to live up to them, we conclude we aren't good enough, not yet anyway. Then not being good enough becomes our self-image, and we get very busy trying to be better. All this striving takes the joy out of life and out of our accomplishments, which in the end, still aren't good enough. There's no end to the perfection and accomplishments the ego demands. We are never done trying to get what the ego wants.

The antidote to striving and suffering is to see that whatever *is*, is good enough. Seeing this, gives us breathing room to be able to respond to the moment more purely, from Essence. How and where is Essence moving us, if at all? We discover the answer to this question by observing what is arising right now. Is there an inspiration or urge to act in a particular way? Essence drives us to fulfill our life through inspiration and urges, not through shameful feelings of inadequacy like the ego does. And Essence doesn't go after the same things as the ego. It goes after what is meaningful to our life plan, which can only be known by paying attention to the Now, not to the ego's rules, desires, and demands.

The ego is a difficult taskmaster. That wouldn't be so bad if what the ego pushed us to accomplish was ultimately meaningful and led to true happiness, but it doesn't. The ego is a false taskmaster, often leading us away from what is most meaningful in life. It drives us unrelentingly and without compassion toward its goals, which are contrary to true happiness. At a certain point, we have to say no to the ego and yes to the Heart instead.

This doesn't mean there aren't times when doing something very perfectly isn't called for. Essence knows when perfection is called for, such as during surgery if you are a surgeon. The ego, on the other hand, demands perfection from nearly every action. And the more we listen to it, the more dictatorial it becomes. Those who have learned to ignore the ego still perform well when they need to.

The ego, with its insistence on perfection, doesn't actually cause us to perform better. When we are identified with it, we are likely to be absorbed in our thoughts. Being inattentive to the moment makes us inefficient and clumsy, and interferes with the spontaneous, right action that naturally flows from Essence. We think the egoic mind is our helper in our tasks, but it is actually unnecessary and even counterproductive. When we are just present to whatever we are doing, without thought, and we allow Essence to act through us, we discover that.

Acting spontaneously from Essence may sound mysterious, but we actually do this all the time. Once we start to notice all the ways we already naturally respond to life, we begin to trust this way of living more, and we begin to live more from Essence and less from the ego. However, to live from Essence, we have to be willing to shift our attention from our thoughts to whatever else is arising in the moment: What actions are you moved to perform? What words are you moved to speak? What opportunities are arising? What information or insights are arising?

Essence doesn't waste time perfecting what doesn't need perfecting or acting unnecessarily (e.g., picking up that last speck of dust). When something needs attention, however, Essence is wise enough to give it attention. Wisdom is inherent in us and operates primarily through our intuition. We don't need the egoic mind to guide us. Wisdom doesn't lie in the egoic mind. All it has for us is platitudes and rules, not real wisdom about what we need to know now. For real wisdom, we have to be in the Now because that's where wisdom comes from. If we are busy listening to the mind's programmed assumptions, opinions, and beliefs, we will miss the wisdom that is always available from Essence.

THE HIDDEN BLESSING IN LIMITATION

With all the talk about abundance these days, I would like to put in a good word for limitation. The experience of limitation, whether it is around money, relationships, success, beauty, health, or anything else, is not a mistake. If we are experiencing limitation, then that's the right experience for now. Limitation is a fact of life, and it will be part of our experience in various ways until we leave the world. Limitation serves a purpose, and that purpose is generally to evolve us in some way. Once that evolution is complete, the limitation is likely to disappear, or what was once seen as limiting will no longer be seen that way.

We tend to take experiences of limitation personally. We either feel persecuted by some limitation or blame ourselves for it. We think we shouldn't be having that experience, and we imagine that life would be much better without it. That's the ego's perspective, and it only brings suffering because it isn't true. If we are having an experience, then we *should* be having that experience. To Essence, life would *not* be better without that experience. It's much truer to see an experience as serving us in some way, as having some benefit. Doing that frees us from the ego's suffering and helps us learn whatever Essence intends for us to learn from it.

Limitation is especially difficult for the ego because the ego is under the illusion that it can make life better. When faced with the sense of powerlessness produced by some limitation, the ego suffers greatly. It is ashamed and angry over not being able to manifest what it wants. So the ego's suffering is two-fold: It suffers over not having what it wants, and it suffers a blow to its identity when it discovers it can't get what it wants.

Such a blow is actually a good thing. The inability to manifest what we want is an opportunity to realize there's something more going on than the ego's goals, needs, perceptions, beliefs, and desires. Something else also has the power to shape life, and that is Essence, which may have intentions that are contrary to the ego's plans. Essence's intentions, unlike the ego's, don't relate to desire-fulfillment, but to emotional and spiritual growth, creativity, developing talents, cultivating love and other qualities, and experiencing for experience's sake. The Oneness is out to experience life through us, and sometimes what it wants to experience and what it intends for us to learn require difficult circumstances, challenges, or limitation.

At times Essence uses limitation to bring about lessons or development or to encourage us to change our course or our thinking. Limitation has great value because it develops our patience, restraint, self-reliance, and other positive qualities. It shapes us in ways like nothing else can. It also motivates us to cultivate talents and skills we might not have developed otherwise. Moreover, limitation often drives us deeper within ourselves and fuels the spiritual search or a study of ourselves. We look into emotional, psychological, and spiritual matters to try to fix our "problem." And when the distractions of the ego can't be indulged in because of a lack of resources, we find other ways to be happy. We learn (hopefully) to be happy with simplicity itself, with this very simple and uncomplicated moment. Limitation and the suffering it causes wake us up out of the egoic state of consciousness. Suffering brings the ego to its knees, and that is a good thing.

Sometimes limitation is created by thinking negatively rather than by Essence. In that case, that is also the right experience. The suffering caused by limiting ourselves may motivate us to free ourselves from our limiting beliefs. Such growth may take more than a lifetime, and often does. However, today, with all the resources for understanding psychology and emotions, people can move through emotional issues and beyond negative thinking much more quickly. Evolution is highly speeded up now due to the information and new healing techniques that are available.

It is when we surrender to what is limiting us that we discover the gifts in that limitation. The struggle against the limitation is what causes suffering, not the limitation itself. If limitation is accepted, there is no suffering. However, acceptance often doesn't come easily because most of us have a deep-seated belief that the limiting condition will remain if we accept it. But quite the opposite is true: Once we accept the limitation, we can learn from it. And once we learn from it, we will be free from it, or at least free from suffering over it.

Once we stop resisting an experience, we discover that it is not all bad, as the ego assumes. Every experience has its advantages, and we can find advantages even in limitation, although the ego isn't what discovers this. Acceptance aligns us with Essence, and then it's possible to experience the limitation as Essence experiences it and to experience Essence's peace, contentment, and joy. Then learning what Essence is trying to teach us through that limitation becomes much easier. It will guide us through our intuition to learn what we are meant to learn and do what we are meant to do in the midst of that limitation.

Happiness can be found even in limiting circumstances if we are very present to the moment instead of to our thoughts, which keep us from discovering the gift in the limitation and any other experience. The ego wants things its way, and since that rarely happens, it is always unhappy. But when we surrender to the way things are, we discover that life is miraculously flowing toward greater goodness, harmony, growth, and love—and those things are what we really want.

To be happy no matter what is going on, we have to want growth and experience more than we want what we want. Once we do, we won't need limitation to teach us, since we will be getting what life is trying to teach us in every moment. When we pay attention to the moment instead of to the egoic mind, life unfolds quite beautifully, without the struggles and suffering the ego creates.

LOVING WHAT IS

Loving and embracing whatever is going on is the only sane choice. The alternative is to reject the way life happens to be showing up and suffer over it. If rejecting reality and arguing with it could change the way things are, then doing that might make sense, but railing against the way things are only makes us miserable. Throughout most of our evolution, we don't realize we have a choice between suffering and not suffering.

We are programmed to listen to the egoic mind, which rejects life. No matter how many things might be just right and very pleasing in any moment, the mind often finds something that *could* or *should* be better and focuses on that. The ego is designed to do that. We don't realize that the ego's voice—the voice in our head—is not a voice of truth and wisdom. It really seems true, and we believe it and assume that what it says is our personal belief. We identify with its point of view and cling to it as if it was true and as if there was no other possibility.

What a blessing it is when we finally see that we don't have to agree with the egoic mind's perceptions, when we see that these perceptions have only caused us to suffer. The ego's point of view is essentially a negative and very narrow one. So much is left out in the stories it tells. The ego rejects and dislikes so much about life. When we agree, or identify, with the egoic mind, we feel negative and small, narrow and contracted.

Why does the ego reject and resist life? Rejecting something gives the false self a sense of existing as somebody with a point of view and a problem to solve, something to do. Then life becomes about improving ourselves and making things better so that life feels better, so that the ego is finally happy and at peace.

But no matter how hard we work to improve ourselves and things around us, we and life still won't be good enough for the ego. It will never rest because to stop rejecting life would mean its death. If the *me* were fine as it is, the *me* would lose all definition, and there would no longer be a sense of a separate *me*. The ego would no longer be in power, and what would be left to run the body-mind would be what has been here all along, breathing and enlivening the body—Essence.

Dissolution of the ego is the goal of the spiritual path, but it is not the goal of the ego, which is opposed to its own termination, not surprisingly. So the ego continues to find fault with whatever is being experienced. The ego doesn't actually die, although it can fall so far into the background that it is barely apparent. When we withdraw our attention from the egoic mind, the ego becomes weak, impotent. It's still there, but it doesn't have the ability to run us and rule us. When the ego is weakened, it becomes much easier to ignore. When we do ignore the mind, we find ourselves in the moment and at peace, no longer struggling against life, but flowing with it.

When we drop into Essence, there is a natural acceptance of life as it is, a feeling of yes to whatever is happening. When we finally agree with life, it is such a relief. Such peace and contentment is what everyone really wants. Usually we experience these feelings when life finally goes our (the ego's) way. Then we relax, until the next thing happens that we don't like.

We don't have to wait for things to go our way to be happy. We can see that things are always going our (Essence's) way, no matter what is happening. The ego's perspective is that life isn't going its way. Essence's perspective is that life is always going just fine. All is well. When we are aligned with Essence's perspective, we are at peace; and when we are aligned with the ego's perspective we are unhappy. It's that simple.

Why would we choose a perspective that brings dissatisfaction over one that doesn't? That's a good question. Most people don't realize they have a choice. Realizing we have the power to choose our perspective is the beginning of freedom. We can choose how we perceive life. We can choose the story we tell about life. The story can be a sad or angry one, or it can be one that allows us to be happy and at peace with life.

Essence loves whatever is happening because it either created it or allowed us (our ego) to create it for our growth and evolution. What we learn to love about whatever we are experiencing is how perfectly it is suited to support our evolution toward greater love, peace, wisdom, compassion, courage, patience, and understanding. Life is perfectly designed to evolve us, and that is what is lovable about every moment.

Whether the ego likes what is happening or not is irrelevant. The ego will like and dislike, feel happy and feel sad, reject and embrace, according to its perceptions. The ego creates feelings of happiness or sadness with its perceptions. These feelings come and go, like the weather, and are simply reflections of the ego's preferences. Happiness that comes and goes so easily is not the happiness we are searching for, because happiness that is so ephemeral will never satisfy us. The happiness that our soul longs for is the happiness that comes from knowing the truth about life and about who we really are. True happiness comes from discovering for ourselves the goodness at the core of life and that life can be trusted. Once we realize that life is good, embracing whatever is happening is easy, because we know that whatever the experience is, it is exactly the right experience, at least for now.

EMBRACING THE MOMENT

The present moment is the only moment we have. The past is over, and the future is yet to be. And when the future does come to pass, it will be experienced as a simple moment, like this one. Even a dramatic occurrence, such as a big win or loss, is experienced only briefly, before it passes away and is replaced by some other experience. The wins and losses of the past are brought into the present moment by the mind, where it attempts to cling to or change what has happened. Attempting to re-experience or alter something from the past causes suffering because it takes us out of the Now and involves us with a desire for something that can't be. The past and even the present moment can't be different than they are because it's already too late for that. To want something other than what is true and real right now causes suffering.

We suffer because our mind either refuses to accept or tries to hang on to something about the past, or because it longs for something that isn't present. When we are in the Now and fully experiencing it without a desire for it to be any different, there is no suffering. The circumstances of the moment are whatever they are, until they aren't, which will soon be the case, since what is showing up in the Now is always changing. We can't maintain suffering, ecstasy, or any other feeling or experience without a lot of mental effort because life keeps moving on.

Grief can last a very long time because the egoic mind reanimates the pain of the past by dwelling on the past and telling sad stories about it that keep the pain alive. Without such stories, fleeting experiences of grief would come and go, like a rainstorm that comes in and swiftly passes. The egoic mind creates emotions, and it sustains them through a repetition of stories. Grief is a natural response to loss, but a loss can only be experienced repeatedly through thought. The loss has already taken place, and a lack of acceptance of it keeps the loss and pain alive. Accepting loss allows us to move on and experience the present moment and what is taking the place of the loss. With every ending, is a new beginning. Clinging to the past makes seeing what is trying to take the place of what is gone more difficult.

Acceptance isn't difficult when you see that the alternative is to suffer. We eventually learn to accept life because the alternative is too painful. Life teaches us to accept what it brings because we suffer if we don't. We come to see that arguing with reality only causes us and those around us pain. It doesn't change reality. This may seem obvious, but it isn't obvious to the ego, which is like a child who demands its way. Fortunately, we are not the ego, but what is able to observe the ego and see that we are causing our own suffering by taking the ego's point of view. When we detach from the ego enough to see this, we are free from its suffering. Then it is possible to surrender to and even enjoy the moment just for what it is.

We can learn to be adventurers in our attitude toward life. We can learn to enjoy seeing what will come next. We can become someone who embraces whatever life brings. Life is always changing, and life can be quite a surprise. When we experience the moment free of the ego's judgments and desires, life becomes interesting and curious. Without a preference for our experience to be other than the way it is, we discover that the present moment is more than alright; it's just right.

GOD IS IN THE DETAILS

One of the reasons we reject being in the Now is we overlook the details of what we are experiencing. Many moments are ordinary and seem similar to other moments we've experienced: We get up and do the same thing every morning, we walk the dog on the same path, we cook the same food, we drive the same roads. To the ego, the routines of life seem boring. It assumes those routine moments are like every other similar moment, so it overlooks what is going on. The ego draws us into thoughts about something else it deems more interesting and exciting. It tries to take us out of the moment and into its world of thoughts, and we are especially willing to identify with it when we are doing something we've done many times before.

The truth is, however, that no moment is the same, and no real joy can be experienced by living in the ego's mental world, where all thoughts refer back to *me* and *how my life is going*. To experience joy, we have to be present to what is real, to what is going on right now. If we assume the Now isn't interesting or worth paying attention to, as the ego does, we won't discover the inherent joy, aliveness, contentment, and value of being in the moment.

When we do allow ourselves to be very present to what is going on, we discover the joy Essence has in experiencing life, including the details of life. The joy is in noticing the light reflecting off the silverware, the specks of dust floating in the sunlight, the contentment on a dog's face, the way the folds of a curtain fall, the shadows cast by the rocks, the clouds changing shapes, the smell of fallen leaves, the taste of butter on bread, for example. If we notice, an infinite variety of things are available in the present moment to enjoy. But we have to be willing to notice the small things, the details, because details are what set one moment apart from all others.

The ego sees something it has seen hundreds of times, and it assumes it knows that thing. The mind might think about it, analyze it, judge it, or just overlook it. It skips over a thing or an experience and substitutes thoughts for experience. In assuming it has already seen that thing or had that experience, the ego misses out on what the moment has to offer, which is where the juiciness and aliveness of life is. The ego's mental world is a dry one. Its world lacks connection with real sensory experience. The richness in being alive comes through our senses. When we experience what is coming into our senses, we feel alive, and we feel the joy that Essence feels in being alive.

When we stop taking the egoic mind's assessment of things as true and start allowing ourselves to have the experience we are having, fully and in great detail, we experience, at last, the happiness and peace the ego promises but can't deliver. The ego offers us its world of thought, but the ego's world comes at a high price. That price is experience. When we give our attention to our thoughts about an experience, we lose touch with the actual experience. We can't really have both the experience and thoughts about it. Our attention is on one or the other, although it can move very quickly between the two.

When we are just present to what we are experiencing, we notice all sorts of sensory details that are usually overlooked. The surprising thing is the amount of joy that can be felt in experiencing the simplest of things fully: the warmth of the sun, the softness of fabric against the body, the brilliancy of the blue sky, the squishiness of the earth below our feet, the scent of a pine tree, the buzz of something in the distance. The ego isn't satisfied with such experiences because it isn't satisfied with anything. We aren't satisfied with such things either when we are identified with the ego because identification with the mind keeps us from fully experiencing them. But what *is* life but the experience of these simple things?

The egoic mind creates a drama out of life. At the center of the ego's drama is the *me*, when life is really just an experience of one simple moment after another. What is experiencing life is no-body, no-thing—the spacious emptiness that is our true nature. Without the mind's interpretations, judgments, fears, doubts, and other overlays onto the present moment, life is a simple sensory experience that is free of problems. That real, sensory experience is more than enough to be happy. In fact, sensing life fully is the secret to happiness.

THERE IS ALWAYS SOMETHING TO LOVE

The alternative to rejecting something about the way things are, which is what the ego does, is finding something to love about it. There is always something to love in every moment. Can you find a sensation, something of beauty, or a sound that is loveable? Is peace here, even just a sliver? Is love? Is contentment? Is the universe holding together?

Being happy or not being happy is largely a matter of what we focus on. The ego can be miserable, and we can still be happy if we find something loveable about what is going on. Finding something to love is hard for the ego, but it is actually easy because there's plenty that is loveable about life. From Essence's standpoint, all of life is loveable because Essence experiences life differently than the ego. Essence says yes to it, while the ego says no. Paying attention to the ego's rejection of life makes us miserable, while noticing what is loveable fills us with love.

The secret to happiness is to love, not to be loved, but to love. Loving is essentially saying yes to life, accepting it. Loving feels good, even better than being loved. Nothing feels better than loving. However, the ego doesn't want to love as much as it wants other things, such as power and security. It would rather feel angry, sad, or any other emotion than love. Emotions give the ego some identity, some reason for existing. They give it a problem to fix. The ego doesn't want to love because loving makes it feel vulnerable. It doesn't trust love because it isn't what creates or experiences love. Loving is the domain of Essence, and when we are experiencing love, we are experiencing Essence. So to move out of the ego and into Essence, all we have to do is find something to love. Doing that is easy, but the catch is we have to want to do it.

The *you* that wants to move out of ego-identification and into Essence is the *you* that is already not identified with the ego. That *is* a catch! The ego doesn't want you to move out of ego-identification, but something else does, and that is Essence. There comes a time in our spiritual evolution when we become aware of a *you* that can choose to move out of ego-identification. Then we begin to wake up out of ego-identification and live more as Essence in the world. Essence is what chooses love over the ego's values. Essence is what loves, not the ego.

When we choose to find something loveable about the present moment, we will find many things. One thing that is always loveable is simply our willingness to love. What a miracle! In the midst of such a painful and difficult world, we have within us a willingness to love. That goodness within us is extremely loveable. That same goodness is within everyone else too, although that goodness—God-ness—is often hidden by the ego. Still, there is much evidence of the goodness within everyone when we look for it.

One of the easiest ways to experience love is to give our attention to something we love. Just looking at our pets, for instance, opens our Heart, which is why pets are such a gift to us. Of course our children and other loved ones also open our Hearts, although their egos and ours often complicate love. Our pets' lack of ego allows our ego to relax and stay in the background. Anything of beauty also evokes our love: nature, colors, art, and music. Since beauty is always available, love is always available.

We can also experience love for the gift of being alive and for being able to experience the present moment. That is the love Essence feels as it lives life through us. What a wonder the physical body is! That sense of wonder and gratitude for life, the body, and other living things is love. The Being that we are is in awe of life. When we move our attention onto that which loves life, we feel complete. Nothing more is needed in the moment than that. What a surprise that life can be this simple and complete!

Finding something to love about every moment is the antidote to the ego's rejection of the moment. When you find yourself struggling against life, stop and notice what is beautiful and loveable. And don't just stop with one thing; find another and another. Life can be lived from a place of celebration and gratitude instead of a place of rejection. It is your choice.

LOVE WHAT YOU DO

One step beyond accepting whatever is happening is loving it. Once we accept what's happening, then we might as well love it. Loving whatever is happening just means getting involved, or absorbed, in it, jumping right into it and having the full experience of it. Thinking dilutes experience and keeps us from fully immersing in whatever we are doing. Thoughts accompany most experiences, and keep our attention from being completely on whatever experience we are having. Whatever you are doing, really do that, jump in with both feet. If you're going to eat that piece of cake, then really experience it, unaccompanied by thoughts of guilt or strategies for how you will make up for the calories.

So often, we commit to doing something without really committing to it. We have one foot in an experience and one foot out of it. While we are doing something, we question whether we want to be doing it, complain about it, or think about something else. Being involved with our thoughts dilutes the experience we are having. It removes us from that experience and makes enjoying it difficult.

If you can't commit to being fully in an experience, then one option might be to not do it at all. Do you really need to do it or do it at this time? The ego pushes us to do things on its timetable and to do things aligned with its goals. It pushes us to do something *and* complains about doing what it's pushing us to do. If you're going to do something, then commit to doing it with joy. If you can't do something with joy, then consider not doing it at all or not doing it just then, if you can.

Any experience can be enjoyable if our attention is fully committed to it. The secret to enjoying life is committing our attention to whatever we are doing. When we do that, we land in the Now and in Essence, and Essence loves life. As long as we continue to give our attention to what we are experiencing, we will feel love for life, however life happens to be showing up.

Giving our attention to what we are doing is much more difficult when we are doing something we don't like to do. If we didn't like doing something in the past, we often assume we won't like doing it again, but do you really know that? The reason we don't like doing something is because the mind gives us reasons for not liking it: Doing it is uncomfortable, messy, hard, tiring, scary, and so on. Such complaints seem reasonable from the ego's standpoint. However, we can love doing something even though it's uncomfortable, messy, hard, tiring, scary or whatever. Besides, no experience can be summed up in a few words. These are the ego's stories, which don't capture the entire, real experience. The mind emphasizes the negatives and ignores the positives. When we focus on the negatives, they become magnified, and the rest recedes into the background. The result is that we have a negative experience.

Essence loves experiences the ego considers unpleasant just as much as it loves pleasant ones. It doesn't categorize life as good or bad, pleasant or unpleasant, like the ego does. It doesn't evaluate or judge like the ego does. "Pleasant" and "unpleasant" are not in Essence's vocabulary. Whatever *is*, is just the way it is, without a particular definition. Accessing the part of us, Essence, that loves the experience we are having is always possible, but to do that, we have to ignore the ego's point of view.

Complaining about something while we are doing it makes it impossible to enjoy it. Check it out for yourself: Has complaining ever improved an experience? What happens when you give up your complaints and become absorbed in the experience rather than in the pain, discomfort, or resistance to it? Without the ego's complaints and fears, even physical pain can be accepted and more easily endured. Without the mind's complaints, enjoying, or at least accepting, anything is possible.

The ego likes to complain because complaining gives it something to talk about. The chatterbox mind has to say something! So the mind finds something it doesn't like and gets very busy building a case against it. The problem is, if we are complaining about something when we're doing it, complaining becomes our experience of doing it, and we're no longer having the full experience of the Now.

To love what we are experiencing, all it takes is our attention. When we give our attention to something, love flows to it. So if you want to love what you're experiencing instead of resist it, give it your attention. That is the antidote to the ego's resistance. If we give our attention to our resistance, we are loving resisting. Then resistance is magnified and becomes our experience.

Because the ego doesn't want to love, we have to find within us that which is willing to love life just as it is. We have to summon that to counter the ego's complaints and resistance to life. We summon, or align with, Essence by giving our full attention to the Now.

DO WHAT YOU LOVE

Here's the secret to happiness: Do what you love. Pretty obvious, you say? Yes! If it is so obvious, why isn't everyone happy? We aren't happy because most of us do what the ego loves and not enough of what Essence loves: We indulge in all sorts of pleasures, shop, and do other fun things. The ego also loves to work. Have you noticed? It works very hard to get what it wants. It also loves getting attention and being special. The ego loves doing different things than the real you, or Essence, and therein lies the rub.

It's not that the real you doesn't love pleasure, fun, thinking, work, and the other things the ego enjoys; Essence just doesn't love them to the exclusion of the other things it loves and values, which are lower on the ego's list. The ego and Essence have different priorities, and their priorities sometimes get in each other's way. When we are identified with the ego, we do too much of what the ego loves and not enough of what Essence loves. That can lead to depression and unhappiness: too much eating, drinking, partying, shopping, thinking, working, pushing, and striving.

So the prescription for happiness isn't to do what the ego loves (although the ego won't agree), but to do what the real you loves, because the real you will also do enough of the things the ego loves, but not too much of them. And the real you won't ignore other more meaningful activities.

What do you love to do? Identifying that can be tricky because we often confuse the ego's desires with Essence's. There's a really good way to tell what the real you loves to do: When you think of doing that, your Heart jumps with joy. Essence expresses itself through the Heart, while the ego expresses itself through the mind, as, "I want..." or "I like...."

What we love to do arises naturally within us and is expressed if we don't let our ego block that impulse with fear or some belief or objection. Such blocking happens all the time when the ego's goals conflict with what is arising from Essence to do. The ego tries to talk us out of following our Heart. To try to convince us of its point of view, it uses fear, doubt, discouragement, and *shoulds*: "You should get a job that pays more." "Your parents will never forgive you if you do that." "You won't be able to pay your bills." "You aren't smart enough."

The ego's fears may even come true, but is that a reason not to follow your Heart? Is anything worth going against your Heart? When we follow our Heart, life does work out; it just may not work out the way the ego wants, although it just might. We don't know what will happen. The truth is that, even if we follow the ego, we don't know what will happen. But if we follow our Heart, then whatever happens, we will feel happy and we won't regret our decision.

What we love and most deeply want to do shows up in the moment as an impulse, inspiration, or urge. We may think about that impulse, inspiration, or urge, or express it verbally, but what makes our Heart sing doesn't show up initially as a thought. What is most meaningful for us to do shows up as a feeling of wanting to do something, not as the thought "I want...." That's the difference.

"Follow your Heart" means follow your feelings. However, those feelings aren't the emotions that come from the ego, but the deeper drives of Essence. We *feel* that something is right or true, and that feeling is an intuition, not an emotion. Following our emotions can get us into a lot of trouble, but following our intuitive feelings brings us happiness and fulfillment.

Essence loves creating, playing, learning, exploring, working, expressing, and growing. It also has more specific things it loves to do through each of us, depending on our talents and the purpose of our life. For instance, if you have a life purpose related to writing, you will love to write, whether or not that brings you fame or fortune. Or if your life purpose relates to parenting, you will love children and long to have them. You will love any activities that relate to your life purpose. You will even love activities that don't relate to your life purpose if they help you accomplish that purpose.

We are programmed to love the things we need to do to fulfill our life plan. What a beautiful and amazing thing that is! If you do what you love, what your Heart desires, you will fulfill your life purpose and be happy. Doing what you love is the prescription for happiness and proof that love is the force behind life.

DO WHAT ESSENCE LOVES

The Creator has a penchant for certain things. It loves to create. It created everything that exists, and it loves to create through us as well. Many life purposes relate to creating, so many people are driven to create. Whether our life purpose relates to creativity or not, everyone loves to create and is creative to some extent. We can't help but create.

Creating comes natural to us because we are like that which created us. Why did this amazing creation we call life happen? It happened because of a will to create, which is also within us. And that drive is very powerful. It is a drive for life, a drive to live and to find out what will happen and what we can make happen. The French call it *joie de vivre*. The joy in living is the joy Essence feels in being alive through us.

What would it be like to be alive and not express ourselves? Expression is natural to us because it is natural to what created us. The Creator, the Oneness, expresses itself through creating, and it expresses itself through us as Essence. The Creator, the Oneness, created us to be unique so that it could have many diverse vehicles to experience life through. Expressing itself through us gives the Oneness great joy, and when we allow it to do that, we feel that joy.

The Creator also loves to learn. It loves to stretch itself. One way it stretches itself is to create challenges for itself to learn from by manifesting a world that requires adaptation and intellectual evolution to survive. Those who survive best learn from life and pass their learning on. That ability to learn and adapt evolves our species. We as individuals evolve, and the species evolves.

All this learning and evolution is very interesting to the Creator. It doesn't know exactly what will happen to its creations after they've been created. It participates in creation through its creations, but within creation is an element of free will that provides a wild card, an unknown variable. Apparently, the Creator also loves the unknown!

The Creator loves the unknown because it loves discovery and problem-solving. It loves to grow and triumph over problems and difficulties. The ego doesn't like challenges, but when we are aligned with Essence instead of the ego, we love a challenge. Perhaps that's why the ego was created. It provides us with the biggest challenge of all: being lost in the illusion that we are separate from what created us. We are programmed to believe this illusion, and our challenge is to see through it. What a puzzle. The Creator must like puzzles.

When we fall in love with life, as the Creator has, we find happiness, joy, and peace. To experience that joy, we may need to do some of the things the Creator, or Essence, loves so much. We need to make time to do what Essence is moved to do through us, rather than being caught up in the ego's goals. The ego can keep us very busy, so busy that we forget to notice what else we are moved to do. Essence isn't as pushy as the ego. Essence reveals its intentions more subtly, and we might miss them if we are busy listening to the mind, or just plain busy.

If we pay attention to the more subtle communications from Essence, we will find ourselves doing more of the things that bring us joy. We may do more dancing, singing, creating, playing, walking in nature, moving the body, resting, being, listening, exploring, being silent, noticing, learning, growing, questioning, looking within, and meditating. The ego doesn't particularly value many of these activities, so we tend to not make time for them, or at least not as much time as Essence might make for them.

If there's any activity we do too much of to the detriment of Essence, it's thinking about ourselves. The ego interferes with joy by involving us too much in thoughts about ourselves and how our life is going. Involvement with the *me* takes us out of the Now and out of the juiciness of life. What if some of these other activities—creating, dancing, singing, walking in nature, exploring, just being, and meditating—replaced some of that thinking? That would dramatically change your world because you would be living more in Essence and less in the ego. What a different life that would be. Would it be so hard to do more of what Essence loves? What would you really lose in exchange for some joy? What really matters to you?

PART 5

Trusting Life

TRUSTING GOD

The God of many of our religions is not an easy God to trust. He is vengeful and punitive, not that we might not deserve it at times. But can you really trust a God that is willing to send his creations to hell for all eternity for displeasing him? Would you, as a parent, do that to one of your children? How can it be that we would be more compassionate than our creator?

An even bigger question is how we can trust a God that creates a world that is full of suffering and provides no explanation for or relief from it, except a promise of heaven if we obey. Is it any wonder why so many people are disillusioned with religion, when it doesn't seem to have the answers for how to be at peace with life, and when over the centuries, through persecutions and wars, religious beliefs may have caused more suffering than they have relieved? We would be foolish to trust the God depicted in most of our religions. Fear him, yes; trust him, no.

Our religions talk about the importance of love, but even many religious leaders don't model love, but intolerance and hatred. So how can we expect their followers to do better? The message of Jesus is to love your neighbor as yourself, but we haven't seen much progress toward that in the last two thousand years. If religions are advocating love instead of violence, it doesn't seem to be working. So what is going on?

There is a loving Intelligence behind all life, but the ego has co-opted much religious thought. It has twisted and warped the truth and made the truth unrecognizable, leaving many people confused and without a sense of being connected to something greater than themselves. It's smart not to trust the God of most religions because that God isn't worthy of our trust. We are too sophisticated to trust such a God. Those who do were indoctrinated early in life and are held in place by the fear of going to hell or some other punishment if they reject the doctrine. Fear is the tool of the ego, and fear is used by many religions to keep their followers from leaving.

The word I like to use for God is *goodness*. God is goodness. If we can't trust the God of our religions, can we trust goodness? Does goodness exist? Are goodness and love at the core of life, or is evil? Both goodness and evil exist in this world of dualities. Goodness is alignment with love, while evil is the absence of love and the result of identifying with the ego. Two forces are at play in the world: the ego and Essence. What prevails will tell us something about what created us and what is behind all life. Is this a world where love and goodness prevail over evil? Is there enough proof to conclude that love and goodness are more powerful and therefore truer than evil? Is the ego God, or is goodness?

We naturally know what is right and good. We don't need religion to define that for us because goodness and love feel one way (they feel good), and hatred and fear feel another way (they feel bad). We have an internal guidance system that points the way to what is right and good if we are willing to pay attention to it. We also have an ego that is out for itself and into getting what it wants, and it's willing to override that guidance system if doing so serves its purposes. Evil is action divorced from love that doesn't recognize the Whole, while love is action that is connected and responsive to the Whole. We have the potential to participate in either type of action. In any moment, we can choose to follow the ego or to follow Essence.

We are never left alone in making this choice. In every moment, we receive encouragement from Essence, our internal guidance system, to choose love over fear and selfishness. Goodness is always vying for our attention, just as the ego is. There is a battle for our souls going on, so to speak. The question is, who is winning the battle? If the world belongs to the ego, the ego would win. If the world belongs to Essence, goodness wins. What do you see happening? Is our species evolving toward love or in the opposite direction?

Based on the violence we see in the news, it may not be obvious that we are evolving toward love. Nevertheless, although there is much evil in the world, as a species, we believe in the value of goodness and love. We don't value oppression and hatred, even though we may behave badly at times. Our values tell us what we are made of, what we come from, and where we are headed.

In your own life, have you evolved toward love or hatred? Hasn't the wisdom you've gained resulted in being more loving and compassionate rather than the opposite? And aren't you trying to be more loving and compassionate?

It is our destiny to move in the direction of love, not in the direction of hatred and fear. Do you know of people who are becoming more evil rather than more loving? It does happen, mostly when someone has been abused or tortured or has suffered some devastating loss. When we have been touched by evil, we can lose our connection to love and become hateful, bitter, vengeful, and mean. But that isn't proof that our species is evolving in that direction.

Evil is a dead end. We can only go so far in that direction before the suffering becomes so great that we realize the need to change directions. Life corrects itself: When we go toward fear, negativity, selfishness, and hatred, we suffer; and when we go toward love and goodness, we stop suffering. This is proof of the goodness—the God-ness—behind all life. Goodness is a God you *can* trust.

WHO YOU ARE IS GOODNESS

Despite the strength of the ego, goodness is stronger and more present in the world than evil. Everyone *has* an ego, but everyone *is* essentially goodness, although that goodness may be obscured by the ego. The ego is the cause of all suffering on this planet. It causes us to suffer within ourselves, and it also harms others, which results in more suffering.

Without the ego, we wouldn't suffer. Calamities would still happen, but we wouldn't suffer over them. We are meant to overcome the ego and our suffering. That is our challenge and what our evolution as humans is about. We are learning to overcome the fear, separation, and suffering caused by the ego and to live in peace and harmony with ourselves, others, and the planet. In short, we are learning to love. Loving is how we return Home to our true nature.

Returning to love is what the journey in third dimension is all about. The journey has a happy ending, and the journey serves a purpose. All the struggle and suffering we've experienced has served us and the Oneness by developing our ability to love. By the end of our lifetimes on earth, we realize that love is all that matters. Then we graduate to other dimensions and existences that are based on service to the Oneness in its many manifestations throughout the universe.

Our suffering teaches us how not to suffer. Once we learn that, we can help others stop suffering. Although suffering is part of this dimension, it is by no means part of every dimension. Beyond our dimension, there is no suffering, only service, learning, and growth. The suffering in this dimension develops our compassion, sensitivity, wisdom, love, patience, and other virtues. The challenge of having an ego shapes us and makes us more capable of serving others now and later in our evolution. That challenge is built into this dimension intentionally because it serves our greater evolution. Having an ego is not a punishment, but grist for our spiritual mill.

The proof of the goodness of life is that we are given a way out of our suffering. We are given resources that help us grow and evolve, and we are given the potential to see through our programming and become free. We are also given way-showers, those who know the way out of suffering. The Oneness doesn't leave us alone to fend for ourselves, even though it may seem that way at times. It has always made available the people, opportunities, and resources we need to grow from our difficulties and overcome our suffering. Not everyone manages to do this easily, but everyone is given what they need to grow.

Because we have free will, we can take as long as we like to discover the truth about life, and many people do take a very long time. They choose the ego and its fear and negativity over goodness for a very long time before they see that goodness and acceptance are the way out of suffering. When they are finally released from entrapment in the ego, they often become the most determined servers. Because they have suffered so much, their motivation to relieve suffering is very great. So even experiencing such pain serves the evolution of the Whole.

We reach a point in our evolution when all that matters is service to life, which we feel intimately connected to as our very own Self. We serve the Whole because serving it feels better than only serving ourselves, as the ego does. Many lifetimes of serving ourselves as the ego taught us the emptiness of doing that. All we got for serving ourselves was suffering, because our self absorption kept us tied to the ego and its discontentment and fear. Getting what the ego wants comes at a very high cost: love and peace. At a certain point, we choose love over what the ego wants.

Goodness is our very nature, and it eventually overcomes the ego's selfishness. Goodness is what wakes us up out of the egoic state of consciousness and brings us Home. It calls us to it unceasingly, and eventually it prevails.

GOD IS GOOD(NESS)

Many people have a hard time believing that God is good when they don't feel that life is good. How can God be good when life isn't experienced as good, but painful? Even though life is essentially good, it is possible to experience it as painful because we are programmed with beliefs that make it painful. The fact that we suffer doesn't make life, itself, bad or painful, even though life can feel that way. We are meant to discover that we create our own suffering by how we think about life and that pain isn't inherent in life.

A lot of things are inherent in life—change, birth, death, aging, illness, accidents, calamities, and losses of all kinds—but these events don't have to be a cause of ongoing suffering. Yes, these events can cause grief and sadness, but grief and sadness pass, like everything else, and are replaced with other experiences. The ego, however, clings to negative thoughts and feelings and, as a result, magnifies, intensifies, and sustains those emotions. Meanwhile, the ego overlooks the subtle feelings of joy, gratitude, excitement, adventure, love, and peace that come from Essence. If we dwelt on such positive feeling states as much as we generally dwell on our negative thoughts and painful emotions, our lives would be transformed. And that is what we can learn to do.

The difficulties and challenges in life aren't proof that life is not good. They are just part of life. For example, the fact that animals eat other animals to survive isn't proof that life is cruel, but just the way life is. The challenges and difficulties we face are not personal.

They aren't proof that we aren't good enough, that we are being punished, or that God doesn't care about us. Challenges are just part of life in this dimension, and part of everyone's life. No one escapes them.

When we don't accept that challenges are part of everyone's life, we suffer. We take life's challenges personally, as if they mean something about us, and they don't. Life's challenges are designed to make us stronger and show us the way out of entrapment in the egoic mind. They are designed to show us the way Home. Life is good because its purpose is good. It supports our evolution, and that evolution is toward greater wisdom and love. Life is wise and loving in providing us with exactly what we need to become free of the egoic mind and return to love.

The way life frees us is by giving us a homing device, which is the love of goodness (God-ness). We all know what goodness is, we all love goodness, and we all have the capacity to express it. When we express goodness, we are rewarded by feeling good and, often, by goodness being returned to us. We know that goodness is at the core of life because it brings us what we have always wanted.

The catch is that our goodness is clouded over by the false self, the ego, the voice in our head that constantly focuses on *me, my life,* and *how it's going for me.* It is primarily a negative voice, which produces negative feelings. It's the only thing that can take us away from expressing our goodness, Essence. It is the only thing in the way! Imagine that—the only thing interfering with expressing goodness (God-ness) in the world is believing and following the egoic mind!

The ego is the Devil, you could say, in the drama taking place on earth. The ego creates suffering, hatred, and every form of negativity. In our search for relief from the ego, we all inevitably discover our essential goodness. What a heroic journey it is! Life isn't easy, but that doesn't mean it is bad. Life is good at its core, and the proof is that we are good at our core. We all eventually discover that, which is more proof that life is good!

TAKING THE LEAP OF FAITH

There are two possibilities: trusting the ego or trusting Essence. There isn't anything else here to trust. In any moment, we are trusting the ego or Essence. Most people are trusting their minds, not Essence, but even they respond to Essence some of the time. Whatever we give our attention to is what we are loving and trusting, and for most people, that is the mind. What makes life so difficult to trust is that the ego doesn't trust life. So if we are trusting the ego, we won't trust life.

Life is difficult for the ego to trust because life is unpredictable. How can we trust something that is so changeable and unpredictable? But does that really make life untrustworthy? Unpredictable, yes; untrustworthy, not necessarily. Does not knowing what is going to happen next mean we can't trust life? What if whatever happened, no matter what it was, served creation, even if we didn't know how? Is that so farfetched?

The ego wants life to serve *it*, but life doesn't do that very well because life serves a higher purpose: the evolution of the Whole. No wonder the ego doesn't trust life to serve it—because life doesn't serve the ego! But, amidst the changeability and unpredictability of life, life is being served, the life of the Whole. We may not be able to understand how an experience we are having is serving the Whole, but that doesn't mean it isn't doing that. Trusting life means trusting that our experiences are purposeful and can be used for the good of the Whole. In retrospect, you can probably see that your toughest experiences were very valuable and changed you in many positive ways, like nothing else could have. When we are in the midst of hard times, we often can't imagine how such difficulties might be serving us. But with time, how they are doing that often becomes clearer.

Believing that our experiences serve us and the Whole helps us benefit from them and move through them more gracefully. That is a better choice than believing life is unfair, cruel, or untrustworthy, not only because it is more beneficial, but also because it's true. When we hold true beliefs, life goes more smoothly than when we hold false beliefs.

One way life leads us Home is by showing us what is true and false: True beliefs feel good and result in happiness, while false beliefs feel bad and result in suffering. When we are aligned with goodness and the positive, life works better than when we are aligned with the ego and negativity. This is how life points us toward goodness and love and away from the ego and suffering.

Trusting life is a huge leap of faith for the ego, one the ego will never take. What eventually decides to trust life is the *you* that is waking up out of the ego. This *you* takes the leap of faith when it is finally so disillusioned with the ego that it's willing to consider another possibility. This *you* can do this because it has gained enough distance from the ego and has had some experiences of itself as Essence. It has tasted Essence enough to know that something else is living life besides the ego.

Leaving the ego and its distrust of life behind is more difficult if we haven't had some experiences of who we really are. If we aren't very familiar with Essence, then we don't know what will take the ego's place. Many people see that they aren't the ego or the mind, but they haven't seen who they really are clearly enough to be willing to move out of ego-identification for very long. Where would they go? The ego tells them there is nothing else, and when they look, what is beyond the ego seems like a Void, like nothing. Who we really are can feel pretty empty and insubstantial and therefore scary when we haven't had a fuller experience of it. That Nothingness can make dis-identifying with the ego frightening until we come to see that something very trustworthy is living our life.

So for most people, moving from the ego to Essence is a gradual process, one of dipping their toe into Essence, running back to the ego, and then back to Essence. Eventually we stay longer in Essence, long enough to begin to trust it. At a certain point, we are ready to take the leap and leave the ego behind, but only when we've had enough experiences of Essence to see that it exists and is worthy of our trust.

THE IMPORTANCE OF EXPERIENCING ESSENCE

We are always experiencing Essence because Essence is who we are, but we may not always be aware of Essence. We take ourselves to be the character we seem to be and all the ideas we have about ourselves. Essence is the ground, or space, within which this character lives. Who we really are is not an entity or a being, but everything, including the space in which everything appears. Who we are is the awareness of everything as well. We couldn't be continually aware of the Oneness that we are because it wouldn't be functional, but we can be aware of the spiritual dimension.

The ego doesn't acknowledge the spiritual dimension because the ego doesn't experience it. Or when the ego does experience the spiritual dimension, it discounts the experience: "Oh that—that's nothing. What good is that?" The ego is only interested in things that can further its goals. When it starts to believe that spirituality has something to offer it, some new way of improving itself, then the ego becomes interested in spirituality. Sometimes the ego takes up the spiritual search, but for its own reasons, not out of disillusionment with its goals.

What takes up the spiritual search for other reasons is the *you* that is ready to awaken. This *you* is possible because it has attained some detachment from the ego and become disillusioned with the ego's goals. At times, the *you* is identified with the ego, but often it is not. In moments when the *you* is not identified with the ego, it experiences Essence—just being—and it comes to love that state of being and wants to experience that state more.

Experiences of Essence drive the *you* forward on the spiritual path in search of more tastes of Essence. Such experiences are very important to the spiritual journey. When we are identified with the ego, we have no sense that another way of living is possible until we have some familiarity with Essence. Encounters with Essence show us that we are something other than the ego, and they motivate us to dis-identify with the ego.

Along the way, the *you* may have some profound and possibly life-changing experiences of the spiritual dimension that solidify the *you's* commitment to discovering the truth about itself and about life. Spiritual experiences feed the spiritual drive and fuel the journey Home. They offer glimpses of the truth that point the way to the truth and motivate the search for it.

Experiences of Essence are available whenever we drop into the Now, but they don't become more common until we welcome them and make room for them in our life. Without some recognition and valuing of such encounters with Essence, we won't experience them as much as is possible. Without some conscious choosing on our part, the spiritual journey will unfold more slowly. But when we choose more consciously to drop into Essence, the journey can unfold more rapidly.

At a certain point, most spiritual seekers feel a deep longing to go Home. That longing strengthens their will to choose Essence over the ego. Meditation is perhaps the most effective and powerful way to invite Essence into our life and learn how to move from the ego into Essence. Through meditation, we discover what Essence feels like, which is important because that experience shows us where we are going. Meditation also gives us practice in getting there and helps us overcome the habit of listening to the mind.

Most people who awaken and become stabilized in that awakeness have practiced meditation regularly, although that isn't universally true. Usually meditation is necessary to prepare the ground for awakening and to be able to maintain a connection with Essence in the midst of life. Experiencing Essence in meditation is one thing, and being able to embody it and live as it is quite another. With sufficient experiences of Essence in meditation, Essence becomes so familiar that it eventually becomes our ordinary state.

There are other ways of getting to know Essence, and those are through other means of altering consciousness, such as dancing, singing, being in nature, playing and listening to music, and creating art. These are time-honored ways of altering consciousness, or dis-identifying with the ego, and becoming acquainted with Essence. Sports that demand our undivided attention also can evoke Essence. Anything that results in a focused mind and helps us move beyond the ego's mental commentary may evoke Essence.

The more experiences we have of Essence and the longer such encounters last, the more our programming to identify with the egoic mind is neutralized. Eventually the programming becomes so weak that it loses its ability to capture our attention. Then it is really possible to live as Essence.

WHAT IS TRUSTWORTHY ABOUT LIFE

We can trust life to be the way it is. What we can't trust is for life to be different than the way it is. In other words, we can't trust life to be the way the ego wants life to be. We can really trust life to be unpredictable, always changing, and challenging. We can't trust life to be predictable, the same, and easy, which is what the ego would like. Because life isn't the way the ego would like it to be, it declares that life isn't trustworthy. But life is just the way it is—and we *can* trust that.

There are a lot of other things we can trust about life that the ego rails against: We can trust we will age and die, for instance. We don't know what dying will be like, but we can trust that death will happen. The ego doesn't like that we age and die or that we don't know what death will be like or when it will happen. The ego wants to know.

The ego's need to know is the basis of much suffering. It wants to know in a universe where little is really known, so wanting to know is bound to cause a great deal of suffering. Such a desire isn't really a desire because it is so unrealistic. It is more like a complaint: "But I want to know!" screams the angry child.

We all have an ego that takes the form of an angry child who throws tantrums whenever life doesn't go its way. That child is never happy because it wants life to be some way other than it is. The ego is a very irrational part of us that makes impossible demands on life rather than accepting the way things are. Quieting the angry child is possible, but we have to speak to it kindly and compassionately and not argue with it. The child is scared of life, and that fear comes out as frustration, anger, and demands. What it needs from us is comfort and assurance that it, the child, will be okay.

This may seem like a ridiculous exercise, but the child resides in the unconscious, and unconscious parts of ourselves can be healed by acknowledging them and speaking to them. Explaining to our inner child that it's okay and safe for life to be the way it is can help us accept and trust life on a more conscious level.

This primitive part of ourselves, the angry inner child, needs reassurance that life is good and safe and that it, the child, can come out and play, in a sense. Without that reassurance, the angry child may sabotage us in ways we may not be aware of: It becomes enraged over little things or keeps us from following our Heart. The angry child is the voice of distrust, and for those who have been wounded in childhood, its voice is strong, and its fear is real: "Life is not okay. The world is not a safe place!"

Agreeing with that angry voice keeps us identified with the ego, which tries to control life and make life safe through its strategies. Following the ego's strategies for safety and security can take up a lot of our energy and cause us to put our energy in directions that aren't satisfying. The inner child is afraid, and to quell its voice, we may do a lot of things we don't need to do. We don't need to do these things because life is actually safer than we presume.

What is so safe about life? If safety means predictability, then life isn't safe, because life isn't predictable. But if safety means that resources are available when we need them, then life is safe. Let's examine this. When you've been in trouble, for instance, when you had a car accident or got sick, were resources available to help you?

The accident, sickness, or some other difficulty was perhaps unavoidable, as they are part of life and can be trusted to be part of life, but did inner and outer resources show up to help you through that difficulty?

Even when we are entirely alone, we have inner resources for dealing with any difficulty. Although we may also be severely challenged by our ego in times of stress, a more positive voice of wisdom is always available to us. Some people are more aware of that voice, but everyone has access to it. In trying times, we often discover the presence and power of that voice, the inner strength that lies within us.

In a crisis or in difficult times, Essence also usually provides us with people who are willing to help. Such assistance is the function of society. A society or community helps its members survive. Societies and communities exist because the goodness (God-ness) within us created them to provide support for the many manifestation of itself. When most people see another person in pain or difficulty, they naturally respond with help. In times of crisis, we can observe many heroic acts that demonstrate this. Never mind those who aren't demonstrating this; the ego will always be strong in some people. The relatively few people who are unwilling to be helpful and generous don't negate the reality of the goodness in everyone.

Something else that is trustworthy about life is our ability to grow and learn from life. Although some people seem to grow or learn very little from life, not growing and learning is actually quite difficult. Not growing requires a lot of resistance and stubbornness. Even the most stubborn individuals eventually do grow, and they may do it quite suddenly at the end of their lives, as they look back on their life. Or growth might happen once they are out of their body and looking back on their life with the help of spiritual guides. If you trust that life is teaching you something, you won't be wrong. We can trust life to teach us, and we can trust life to teach us through challenges. What we can't trust is that we won't have challenges and we won't have the pain of growing.

When we expect life to be the way it is—unpredictable, changeable, challenging, and full of growth—then life is absolutely trustworthy. Life is perfectly trustworthy in these ways. Essence has designed life to be this way, so it has no problem with life being this way.

We experience peace and acceptance when we drop into Essence and out of our egoic mind, which is the only thing that distrusts life. The ego distrusts life only because it doesn't accept that life is not about fulfilling its desires and dreams, but about something much more profound and wonderful. Life is about evolution and, more specifically, about our evolution toward love and away from fear. For providing that evolution, life is totally trustworthy.

SEEING LIFE AS IT IS

If we are not seeing life as it is, then trusting it is hard. Life seems untrustworthy because it doesn't fit our picture of what life should look like. The ego sees life in black and white, as good and bad. It doesn't see life as it is, which is always quite a mixture of what the ego considers good and bad. Essence, of course, doesn't categorize life. Life just is what it is. When we see life as it is and accept the way it is, we are happy and at peace.

Once we realize that life is never going to fully please (or displease) the *me* that we think we are, we can relax. The ego says, "This displeases me," and leaves out what does please it. Or the ego says the opposite, "This pleases me," and leaves out what displeases it. Either way, the ego leaves out half of the truth. The ego does this to build a case for changing something because that's what egos were created to do—to reject life and then try to fix it. If we pay attention to the ego, we will experience the ego's version of life, which is one-sided.

The truth about life is that it is many-sided. Life doesn't fit into a simple description, or story. No story tells the tale of an experience fully. Every story leaves out so much: other elements of the experience and other possible perspectives on it. The ego views an experience from one angle and takes that as the truth about it. But one version of an experience is not the whole truth, even if many other people (egos) agree with that version.

The truth is that every experience is both challenging and wonderful. There isn't an experience that doesn't have something challenging about it, and there isn't one that doesn't have something wonderful about it, whether or not that is apparent. A wedding day is a perfect example: It is expected to be a wonderful experience, but the reality is that the wedding day can be very challenging. Or take the example of surgery: Surgery is expected to be challenging, but the love and care we receive from others and the gratitude we feel for being alive and for receiving help can make the experience quite wonderful.

Life can shift very quickly between joy and challenge, love and fear, tension and relaxation, and pleasure and pain. Such experiences may even be present simultaneously within the same moment. Our experience never remains the same for long, and every moment is a mixed bag.

When we are able to notice the rich complexity that is present in each moment and each experience, it's possible to rejoice in life, feel gratitude for it, and enjoy the mystery of not knowing what will happen next. How will life show up in the next moment? What will be the ingredients of that moment? And then what? When we are in the Now, that is how we feel about life and how Essence feels about being alive through us.

Seeing life as it really is—as a mixed bag—allows us to trust life because life is predictably a mixed bag. We can expect, or trust, that every moment will be a mixture of things that please the ego and things that displease it.

Every moment is a many-faceted and unique experience. Essence loves the uniqueness and un-categorizable-ness of each moment, which makes each moment rich and precious. Essence savors the unique flavor of each moment, while the ego struggles to take a stand against each moment and tell a story about it. Essence relaxes into each moment, while the ego prepares itself for a fight. Even the ego's argument with life, which goes on in nearly every moment, is a delight to Essence.

Seeing life as it really is allows us to relax. What a relief! We can finally give up the fight against life because it is not a battle worth fighting, and we will never win. Life is the way it is, and acceptance is the only way to peace and happiness. Once we accept life, we begin to flow with it more, and we see how trustworthy it really is. Life is trustworthy not only because we can trust it to be the way it is, but also because the way it is, is good, and because it is taking us toward greater goodness, love, and freedom. It is our destiny to express our goodness, to love, and to be free of suffering. That is the happy ending to this story of evolution. So life must be very trustworthy, after all, when where it takes us is where we've wanted to go all along.

GETTING AND GIVING

The ego is always trying to get something for itself from others and the environment because it is afraid and unhappy. It believes it doesn't have enough to be happy, so its strategy is to withhold what it has and try to get more of what it thinks it needs to be happy. This strategy may seem sensible—and to the ego, it *is* sensible. However, the real solution to the perception of not having enough is to see that that perception is erroneous and that we have always had enough to be happy. Right now, we are existing and being supported in that existence, which has always been true and will be true until we leave the physical plane. From the place of realizing we have what we need to be happy, and only from that place of completeness, giving can happen, because if we believe we don't have enough to be happy, why would we give?

The ego's belief in not having enough blocks love, which is essentially an outflow of attention, energy, or material gifts to others. When the majority of people believe they don't have enough to be happy, the global flow of love and energy is sluggish. However, when the majority of people believe otherwise, love and energy flow, proving the abundance and support that is available in life. Through giving is how the Oneness provides for and takes care of itself in its various manifestations.

We are free to choose the ego's way and withhold what we have to give or to give more freely. The result of these two choices is very different: When we give freely, we feel full and complete; when we withhold, we feel small, petty, impotent, and lacking. We are meant to learn that giving ful-fills us, while withholding and trying to get causes us to feel empty and even more needy. This understanding runs counter to our programming, which drives us to try to get something from others to fulfill our neediness, only to end up even more needy, grasping, lacking, and unfulfilled.

The value of giving is one of the great secrets of life. Giving requires a leap of faith, an ability to trust that giving is worthwhile. Once we begin to trust this and see the results of giving, then giving becomes much easier, even when we feel we don't have enough. To make this leap, we only need to see that the feeling of not having enough isn't true, but merely the way the ego sees life. Feelings don't tell the truth about life, but are an outgrowth of the programming of the false self.

Allowing the perception of lack to interfere with giving results in the very sense of lack the ego believes in. The ego's belief in not having enough is a self-fulfilling prophecy. As long as we believe we don't have enough to be happy, we won't give and we won't discover the truth, which is that Life is abundantly providing for us to the extent that we join the global flow, the outpouring of giving. If we hold ourselves separate from the Whole, however, then we won't benefit as fully from the flow of Life as possible. Life is calling to us to jump into the flow of abundance and to contribute our share. The more who do that, the more abundantly we all can live.

PART 6

Making the Most of the Moment

MAKE THE MOST OF LIFE

We are all so powerful. We have the power to make the most out of life, out of the moment, or to make life unpleasant. The moment is what it is, and what we bring to it makes it either enjoyable or stressful and unpleasant. We are meant to discover that we are powerful creators, if not of our entire reality, at least of our *experience* of reality. We aren't responsible for what each moment holds, but we are responsible for our experience of each moment because we have the power to make any moment heaven or hell. We don't create our entire reality, since other forces are at work, but how we think about and interact with reality (what's showing up in the moment) affects it to some extent and, surely, affects our experience of it.

How much enjoyment can you squeeze out of the present moment? What if that was your job, your aim, your sole (or soul's) purpose? What if you approached each moment with this intention? If you were determined to get enjoyment out of every moment, you would do whatever it takes. What it takes is not listening to negative thoughts, yours or anyone else's.

Disregarding negative thoughts isn't hiding our head in the sand, but simply not allowing the negative to clutter and influence our experience of the present moment. Although we are programmed to think our negative thoughts, worries, and fears serve a useful function, the moment is never helped or improved by negativity. Focusing on negativity and fears doesn't make anyone a better person, nor does it help us function better in the world. In fact, the opposite is true.

How do you squeeze enjoyment out of a moment? For one thing, pay attention to it—closely. Notice what you are experiencing internally, intuitively, and through your senses. Notice the experience you are having, without evaluating and reflecting on it. The mental voice that comments on life and on experience isn't useful or wise. That voice is an impersonator, a false self, and it has nothing to offer. Don't listen to it. When you do, the juice and joy are sucked out of life.

Enjoying life is a matter of recognizing that which is "in joy," which is the Being that we are, Essence. The Being that is living our life is in joy and enjoying every moment. It is rejoicing in the experience it is having, regardless of what that experience is, because this Being has no judgments or stories to tell about any experience or anything. It is just in joy all the time.

We have the power to experience this joy or to disregard it and, instead, experience our mind's stories and judgments about the moment, our mind's endless commentary. We are powerful enough to recognize which choice brings more joy, and we are powerful enough to be able to choose that. If we see we are making choices that don't make the most out of the moment, we can choose differently. When we choose to experience the present moment instead of the mind's commentary about it, our experience of life changes.

So let your guiding question be, "How can I get the most enjoyment out of this moment?" Although seeking enjoyment from the moment might seem self-serving, seeking the Heart's joy is actually the most selfless thing you can do, because to experience enjoyment, the false (selfish) self must disappear. And the Self that remains is supremely serving itself—the whole of life—through you.

I'D RATHER BE FISHING

Resistance to what we are doing is often caused by a subtle sense that doing something else is more important or necessary. Subtly, unconsciously, we diminish in our minds the importance of certain activities, such as picking up around the house, taking the dog out, taking a shower, or going to the grocery store, as if these activities weren't part of life, or shouldn't be. We move through many routine activities unconsciously, without being present to them, and often with resentment or a feeling that they are causing us to miss out on something more worthwhile, meaningful, or fun. What we don't realize is that not bringing our full attention to the activity, or not being present to it, is the cause of our discontentment or boredom with it, not the activity itself.

Since we probably won't get any excitement or sense of being special from performing routine activities, the ego discounts them and thinks of them as things it has to do but doesn't want to do. So the ego tends to resist ordinary tasks or rush us through them. But life isn't designed for the entertainment, pleasure, and bolstering of the ego. Life is what it is, and the value of life and of what we do isn't adequately measured by the ego's standards.

Essence loves everything about life and embraces each minute equally, without evaluating an activity as worthwhile or not. We can't really miss out on life as long as we are present to it, however it happens to be showing up. We only miss out on life when the ego takes us away from being present to whatever we are doing because it deems it unworthy of our full involvement and attention.

Thinking of some activities as worthwhile and others as not causes us to be dissatisfied with much of what is experienced and needs to be done. Most moments are taken up by mundane activities and duties, and few provide the ego with the excitement and boost to its self-esteem that it lives for. If we are waiting for the kind of moments the ego wants in order to be happy, we will be waiting a lot, which is how life feels when we are identified with the ego. Those few exciting moments the ego is waiting for will fly by as quickly as every other moment, and we will be left once again in this ordinary, unglamorous—but beautiful in its own way— moment.

Every moment has the beauty we long for if we are willing to notice that beauty. Essence sees the beauty in everything, while the ego glides over everything it has seen before as if those things didn't exist. The ego discounts what it sees, while Essence really sees what it sees. When we are aligned with Essence and really see something, we experience an opening of our Heart and a loving of what we are seeing, no matter what it looks like. And when we are aligned with Essence and really involve ourselves in doing something, whatever we are doing is surprisingly pleasurable! The ego has its ideas of pleasure, but those ideas are only occasionally met by life. Meanwhile, the ego misses out on the pleasure and beauty that are available in anything we do, if only we give it our full attention.

DO WHAT'S IN FRONT OF YOU

Living from Essence is often a matter of doing what's in front of us: If something needs picking up, you naturally pick it up. If someone shows up who needs help, you offer it. If dishes need washing, you wash the dishes. If a job needs to be done, you do it, one step at a time. Or if you need to rest, you rest. Or if you need to eat, you eat. The mind complicates life with a lot of thoughts about how, when, why and whether to do various things. It plans and thinks about doing things, when life is simpler than that.

Much of the time, living is just a matter of doing what arises to be done. Life calls on us to take action: Phones ring, children ask for assistance, dog's look at us longingly, email arrives, papers arrive on our desk, the refrigerator is empty, the laundry basket is full, ideas and inspiration arise. We may think that our ego and conditioning are responsible for accomplishing what we do in a day, but the ego doesn't actually do anything. (How can it, when it doesn't even exist?) The ego only *thinks* about doing things: It debates, pushes, resists, complains, and worries about whatever arises to be done. Meanwhile, we do what we do. We choose whether our doing is in response to the egoic mind or follows naturally from Essence.

What to do in any moment is complicated by the mind's resistance, worries, and complaints and by its going over plans of the future and events of the past. All this thinking takes quite a bit of energy. What to do in any moment is also complicated by feelings, which the ego is also responsible for. Feelings also take time and energy away from just moving through life. When feelings arise, they seem like a problem to solve. And the way the egoic mind thinks about things creates even more seeming problems to fix and things to do, many of which don't need to be done.

One reason people feel overwhelmed by life is they expect to be able to do everything they *think* of doing. But thinking is a lot easier than doing! Doing takes time, and thinking takes no time in comparison. We tend to compare how we want things to go with how long something actually takes, and then we feel like we don't have enough time. But we always have enough time for whatever we are doing—because we're doing it! We may not have time for what we *think* about doing, because we can think about doing so much. The mind is always jumping ahead to other things while we are doing whatever we are doing, and that leaves us feeling like there's never enough time. It leaves us feeling hurried and harried, when all that's being asked of us is right in front of us. That's all we can do anyhow.

When we take the present moment just for what it is, life is very manageable. The only thing that makes it unmanageable is thoughts, which ironically are an attempt to manage life. The mind's attempt at managing life takes us out of the Now and makes us feel unhappy, tense, and less efficient. We don't need that voice in our head that tries so hard to orchestrate our every move and fill up our time with activity and busy-ness.

With its thoughts about the past and future, the egoic mind creates a sense of time and then causes us to feel there isn't enough time. The ego is a time tyrant. Being in the present, on the other hand, without the mind's tyranny, is a timeless place of enjoying whatever we are doing, no matter what that is. Since we can only get so much done in any moment, we might as well enjoy what we are doing. Listening to the mind doesn't help us accomplish more; it only makes us feel inadequate, stressed, and discontent with whatever we are doing.

Once you see that listening to the egoic mind is dysfunctional rather than functional, it becomes easier to ignore the mind's tyranny—its pressuring, evaluating, to-do list, and worries. Such thoughts don't serve you and never have. You can be done with them, and you'll get as much done as ever, or you'll discover that some of what you *thought* you had to do wasn't necessary. You also discover that there's room in the present moment to just rest and be.

Once the egoic mind stops ruling us, we finally get what we have been striving for all along: the feeling of having arrived. Where we arrive is in the peace and contentment of the Now. We will never feel peace and contentment if we listen to the mind, and we will never get to where the ego is pushing us because there is no end to its pushing.

FINDING PLEASURE

The ego is all about pleasure-seeking, and the ego does find pleasure. But just how much pleasure and at what cost? In the ego's world, pleasure-seeking too often turns into regrets, as we continue to go after something that gives us pleasure long after the pleasure has ended. Eating is a good example of how unsatisfying too much pleasure seeking can be: Many of us eat for pleasure until we feel sick. Where's the pleasure in that? The ego doesn't know when to stop.

When you are identified with the ego and in pleasure-seeking mode, are you really enjoying whatever pleasure is there? Are you really enjoying the food you are eating? How aware are you of the flavors and the actual experience? When we are very identified with the ego when we are eating, we barely notice the food going down. The ego is goal-oriented even around food, and its goal is to get done eating in order to have more. Is there really that much pleasure in that? When anything is done in excess and without being present to it, which is generally how the ego pursues pleasures, that experience isn't as pleasurable as it could be.

It's funny that we generally think of pleasure as unspiritual, wrong, or sinful (according to religious conditioning), when pleasure is built into life. We can't be alive and not experience pleasure. Apparently, we are meant to experience it. Is it possible that pleasure is one of the intentions of the Creator in manifesting this dimension? One of the benefits of creation is that the Creator, through us, gets to experience pleasure, along with everything else. Pleasure is good!

The more we go in the direction of Essence and away from the ego, the more pleasure we experience, because pleasure is largely dependent on how present we are to whatever we are doing. Anything can be pleasurable if we are present to it without the interference of the egoic mind. The simplest things are pleasurable when we are present to them, even things we generally don't like. Being present is one of the secrets to happiness. The more we drop out of our egoic mind and into our senses, the more pleasure our senses deliver. Pleasure actually points the way Home.

It is ironic that the ego goes after sensual pleasure, while at the same time it keeps us out of our senses and involved with thoughts. Involvement with thoughts interferes with any sensual experience— just try reading and eating at the same time. We can't be mentally engaged and engaged in our senses at the same time. We are doing one or the other, which means that if you are thinking, you aren't going to be fully present to whatever else you might be experiencing. Ego-identification is identification with thought— often negative thoughts—so being identified with the ego actually interferes with pleasure.

Learning to move out of the egoic mind and into the experience we are having is an important step in our spiritual evolution because this simple act is a movement away from the ego and into Essence. Real pleasure is available in every moment by simply being present to whatever we are experiencing. Life rewards us with pleasure when we are present to what we are experiencing, which is how Life brings us Home. Because the ego's pleasure-seeking doesn't ever satisfy, we begin to realize that the ego keeps us away from the real pleasure of just being alive and experiencing life through our senses, which are heightened when we aren't paying attention to thoughts or when thoughts have stopped.

The pleasure the ego offers is faint in comparison to the pleasure of being present, but we don't find that out until we give being present a real try. It takes practice before being present becomes as pleasurable as it can be. The more you learn to be present to the experience you are having, the happier you will be, not only because you are free of the egoic mind's negativity and problems, but also because being present is inherently pleasurable. So if you are going to seek pleasure (and why wouldn't you?), look where it can really be found: in what you are experiencing now.

WAITING

The ego is always waiting for something: a relationship, news about something it wants, a vacation, a promotion, a meeting, a move, or some other anticipated change. There's always something just around the corner the ego is looking forward to or hoping to experience that will presumably make life better. This perpetual state of waiting leaves us with a sense that something is missing *now*. But aren't some of the things you waited for in the past here right now, along with a lot more?

What *is* here doesn't matter to the ego because it is focused on what *isn't* here, which is just what the ego is programmed to do. It is programmed to be future-oriented, not present-oriented. The trouble with being identified with the ego is that being future-oriented doesn't feel good. We imagine feeling good in the future when we get what we want, but the actual experience of waiting and wanting something other than what's here is a state of contraction and discontentment. Just notice how waiting and wanting feel in your body. Desires make us feel tense and tight, dissatisfied and unhappy.

Along with tenseness and discontentment, waiting for something feels like an emptiness, a hole, that needs to be filled. That sense of lack isn't a very pleasant feeling either, so we often try to fill that emptiness up with food or other forms of pleasure. If we feel unhappy and like something is missing, the ego's solution is to try to feel good to make up for what's missing, which leads to pleasure-seeking and escapist activities, and those ultimately result in feeling worse. The hole can never be filled this way. The only thing that can satisfy the sense of lack is to drop out of the egoic mind and into Essence, where the juiciness of the real moment can be experienced.

The trouble with thinking about the future is that the future isn't real. It doesn't exist except as an idea. If we are giving our attention to the future, we are giving it to an unreal idea. We are giving our attention and energy to something that has no value and doesn't serve us in any way. The ego won't be convinced that thinking about the future isn't worthwhile, however. It believes such thoughts can create the future, or at least help it cope with the present, neither of which is true.

Thinking about the future keeps us out of the present, where life is happening. When we are thinking about the future, we miss out on what life is showing us right now, which might have value for the future. Maybe an intuition or insight is arising that will inspire action in a profitable or fulfilling direction. If we are paying attention to our thoughts, we might miss any guidance or wisdom that might be coming out of the Now. The ego has lots of advice and guidance to offer, but its advice is informed by conditioning, which is only so helpful. What is true and wise can only come from our depths, from Essence, not from the egoic mind, which merely pretends at knowing.

Once you begin to notice how the ego causes dissatisfaction and emptiness by creating a sense of waiting for something else to happen, you can learn to be present to that sense of waiting. In doing so, you can become free of the suffering caused by waiting and wanting something to happen. The sense of waiting for something better will always be there because the ego produces that feeling constantly. Just notice that feeling and recognize it for what it is. It is just the ego's way of coping with life. Don't identify with that feeling of waiting, that is, don't believe you will be happy when something else happens. You can be happy right now, and all it takes is seeing that happiness doesn't depend on something happening in the future.

Happiness isn't dependent on anything. It is our natural state. When we are quiet, still, and receptive, happiness bubbles into our awareness. It has always been here, but we have to notice it. We won't be able to be aware of it if we are giving our attention to thoughts about the future instead. Turn your attention to what is happening now, and you won't need anything to be different to be happy.

Now is enough. There is nothing missing when we are really present to what *is* instead of to our thoughts. Our thoughts are the only thing that insists that what is here right now isn't enough. Turn away from those thoughts and voila! Nothing is missing. Everything is just as it is meant to be—and that is the truth. Just rest in that realization. All is well and unfolding exactly as it needs to. Knowing this, is the source of peace.

WHAT KEEPS YOU FROM BEING HAPPY?

The only thing that can keep us from being happy is a thought. What a revolutionary truth that is! The kind of thought that interferes with happiness the most is a thought of lack, which is at the base of all desire. If we didn't think that something was missing or lacking about ourselves, someone else, our situation, or life, we wouldn't be unhappy. Unhappiness is caused by believing that something we think we need to be happy is missing. It is this *belief* that makes us unhappy, not the fact that something is or isn't here right now.

The ego produces thoughts of lack. The sense of lack created by the belief that something is missing produces a desire, which is simply the thought "I want." That desire is fed by more thoughts about what getting what we want or not getting what we want will mean. Then feelings, such as fear, come up related to not getting what we want, and action is taken to try to fulfill the desire and waylay any fears.

When desires are pumped up this way, they seem very real and important. We really believe we need what we desire to be happy or safe. That sense of lack makes the world go around, often in a not-so-happy way. But desire and the actions that follow from desire bring us the lessons and experiences we need to evolve. The sense of lack is also at the base of human suffering, and that suffering is totally unnecessary.

What do you believe is missing now? Take a moment to answer this question. The answer to that question is the source of any suffering you may be feeling. What if you didn't believe you needed that to be happy, safe, or secure? Without that belief, you would drop into Essence, which experiences life as a blessing—and as trustworthy. Life provides what we need, although what it provides may not always be what the ego wants. Providing everyone with what their egos want would be impossible. What would a world like that look like? The Intelligence that we are provides each of us with what is necessary for the Whole to evolve and expand.

If we look with Essence's eyes, we can see how beautifully life has provided for us, even when it has brought us challenges. Along with every challenge, life makes available opportunities, resources, and helpers. Do you notice the grace, the goodness, and the support that life offers and has supplied? The ego doesn't notice the bountiful love that is present. It only notices lack because the ego's role is to create problems and discontentment so that we stay involved with the mind. The egoic mind is the central challenge in life that we are meant to overcome. We are meant to see that the egoic mind, which we are programmed to trust, is untrustworthy and that it is the source of unhappiness.

We don't attain happiness by striving for what the ego wants. Striving is painful, and achieving what we want brings only fleeting happiness before discontentment sets in again. No one has yet to attain happiness, because happiness is a state, our natural state. It is discovered, not attained, by moving beyond the egoic mind, by seeing through the mind to the truth about who you are.

Who you really are is alive here and now. It is living your life, and the ego just pretends to be you. When you drop out of the egoic mind, or step back from it, you discover that the only thing that has ever caused you to feel unhappy is a thought. What a blessing it is to discover this, because thoughts can be ignored, and we have the power to do that. We are powerful, not victims of life, but creators, or co-creators, with the One Intelligence that we are. When we stop paying attention to our thoughts, we discover the happiness that is here and has always been here.

HOW DO YOU CREATE STRESS?

The world is stressful—or is it? People feel stressed, but is the world creating stress, or are we creating it by how we think about ourselves, our life, and others? It is possible to be in this busy world, to accomplish what we need to, and to not feel stressed. We can actually accomplish a lot more when we are not feeling stressed.

Stress is a sign that we need to stop a moment and examine what we are saying to ourselves. It is created by a negative thought about what we are doing or about something else, such as the past or the future, a judgment, or a *should*. Not being present to what we are doing but, instead, being identified with our thoughts about what we are doing or about something else causes stress because most thoughts generated by the ego are negative. Negativity causes the contraction in our body and in our energy that we call stress.

Stress is the sense of contraction that happens when we believe the negative stories our mind is telling us about ourselves, life, other people, the past, or the future. The irony is we think we need such thoughts to function when, in fact, they interfere with handling life and make whatever we're doing less enjoyable. Stress isn't caused by circumstances, although it often coincides with some circumstance or event. It simply comes from the negative interpretation the mind gives life in its ongoing commentary about life.

The aspect of the mind that comments on life is the egoic mind, and it is unnecessary. We don't need the egoic mind to function. It masquerades as you, but it isn't you. You are what is actually living life and noticing the mind that is having a problem with life or, rather, making a problem out of life. Once you realize that you aren't the mind that is having a problem with life, then—guess what!—you don't have a problem anymore. There's something else present that isn't having a problem with life, and that's what, or who, you really are. When we align with that, we can be happy and stress-free regardless of what is going on.

So how do you create stress? What does your mind tell you that causes you to feel stressed? Maybe it tells you that you aren't good enough. Maybe it tells you that you aren't doing something fast enough. Maybe it lists all the things you still have left to do. Maybe it tells you that you will never be a certain way or you will never have certain things. Maybe it reminds you of unhappy things that happened in the past. Maybe it imagines being unhappy in the future. The list of what the mind might say is endless.

Notice what your mind says that causes you to feel stressed and unhappy. Everyone's mind has certain favorite "tunes" it plays repeatedly. What's playing on the radio station of your mind today that is causing you to feel stressed? Is it the "Hurry Up" song, the "There's Never Enough Time" song, the "I'm Not Happy" song, the "Everything's Terrible" song, or the "It Shouldn't Have Happened" song?

Notice the relentlessness of some of the mind's messages. Its radio station is undoubtedly one you would turn off if you could. Since you can't turn off this commentary, what can you do? You can get really involved in what you're doing rather than listening to the mind. You can "turn down the volume" by not giving the mind your attention. Instead, give your attention to what you are doing and experiencing and to what is arising within you that is truer and more positive than the mind's commentary.

There's another more positive station to tune in to, which is broadcast from Essence. It sends out signals and messages that guide us in a direction that will make us happy. It also sends out positive feelings, such as peace, love, gratitude, and encouragement that can counteract the negative thoughts and feelings of the ego. We know when we are tuned in to that station because we feel relaxed, at peace, content, and accepting instead of stressed. So why stay tuned to a negative station when another one is available?

Essence's channel may not come in as clearly as the ego's channel at first because Essence communicates more subtly and not as loudly as the ego. But as we get better at tuning in to Essence's channel, the signal gets stronger, and the egoic mind's chatter becomes softer. One channel is the Stress Channel and the other is the Peace Channel. We really do have a choice about what we listen to.

The Peace Channel can only be heard when we are present in the moment, when we are in the Now. To tune in to the Peace Channel, all we have to do is *be, experience, notice,* and *naturally respond* to what is arising in the moment. To tune into the Stress Channel, we just have to start believing our thoughts again. The great news is we have control over our level of stress. Eliminating stress is just a matter of tuning out the negative and tuning in the positive and just being, experiencing, and dancing to that music instead of to the mind's chatter.

EVENTS DON'T CHANGE EXPERIENCE

When something good or bad has happened, that event doesn't change the experience of the present moment unless we bring the memory of it into the moment as a story. For example, if you win a gold medal, that moment of triumph disappears and is replaced by another moment. Unless you bring the memory of winning a gold medal into the present moment, the present moment is just what it is. Even if you do bring that memory, or any other one, into the present moment, that memory can't change the moment fundamentally, although bringing it into the moment will change your *experience* of the moment by taking you out of it and into your reverie about that triumphant time. Even a great memory like winning a gold medal is only so pleasurable and, in fact, lacks the juice and aliveness that the actual experience, or any experience, has. Memories just aren't a good substitute for real life, which is what is showing up *now*, not what showed up in the past or what might show up in the future.

When something we don't like happens, that event also doesn't change the experience of the present moment unless we bring thoughts about it into the present moment. For example, if you are diagnosed with cancer, that moment would likely be very surprising and sad. But then life moves on to the next moment and the next. Unless you bring the story "I have cancer" into the present moment, you are, in a sense, cancer-free, and the present moment is just what it is. There may or may not be physical pain in the present moment, but it can be free of the emotional pain created by the story "I have cancer" and by any of the other sad stories you might tell yourself as a result of that diagnosis. The moment is just what it is, whether we won a gold medal yesterday or found out we had cancer. We are still just here in the midst of whatever is arising now.

Primarily, the experience of any moment is a sensory one if we aren't identified with the stories the mind brings into the moment, which create suffering. Emotional suffering doesn't have to be part of any moment. Suffering is caused by the egoic mind, by thoughts *about* life, not by life. If we are just in the Now, the ups and downs of life don't affect us because we aren't bringing the story of the "up" or "down" into the present moment. All we have is the present moment and what is showing up *now*.

You can be the richest person in the universe or the poorest, but without the story "I'm the richest/poorest person in the universe," who are you? You are just here in the Now, doing whatever needs to be done. The richest person in the universe and the poorest have the same potential for experiencing the present moment and the same potential for receiving joy from it if they don't bring their self-images and stories ("I'm rich." "I'm poor") into it. Nothing is fundamentally different between these two individuals except their stories and self-images. Such stories and self-images make up the false self and are the only thing that can cause suffering. By the way, "I'm rich" can cause as much suffering as "I'm poor" because of the fear of losing one's wealth and because of the separation from others and from life that "I'm rich" can cause. The circumstances of these two individuals are different (everyone's are), but their circumstances aren't what affect their experience of the moment, but rather their thoughts and feelings *about* their circumstances.

In this moment, without all your stories and self-images, who or what are you? You are just this that is having an experience of the present moment. The miracle is that *this* is the same in every individual. What you really are is what everyone else is too. Our ideas and self-images create a false identity, a costume, that we wear and bring into the moment, which colors our experience of it. When thoughts are stripped away, all we have left is life living itself *now*, and that's all that has ever been going on.

WHAT STORY ARE YOU RELATING TO?

We bring a story into nearly every moment, and doing that affects how we experience that moment and how we respond to life. If the story is "I hate washing the dishes" and we are washing the dishes, our experience of washing the dishes is affected by that story. We also might say or do something in response to hating to wash the dishes, such as get mad at someone who isn't helping us with the dishes. We might even throw a dish if the feeling is strong enough.

We also tell stories about our loved ones, such as: "You don't care about me." "You're not attractive enough for me." "I can't live without you." "I need someone more exciting." "I'm not rich enough for you." "I can't see myself with you." We all know what these stories are because they are the kind of "insights" we might share with a friend or someone else we are close to. These stories, the more they are repeated and reinforced, interfere with being present to the people we love, and they are never the complete truth. Rather than responding to our loved ones purely, we let our view of them or our view of the relationship, our story, affect how we react to them. Telling stories and reacting to our stories is going on most of the time unconsciously. We aren't naturally aware of our stories or examine them until perhaps they cause so much trouble that we are forced to.

Our stories about loved ones are created by the ego to strengthen itself, to make the ego look good, or to maintain its beliefs about itself. As a result, they are nearly always detrimental to relationships. The ego tends to spin negative stories about others, not positive ones. Replacing your negative stories with positive ones, or no story at all, can transform your relationships. For instance, what if the story you told about your partner was that he or she is the ideal partner for you? We often tell that story in the beginning of a relationship, but before long, the ego begins spinning its negative stories. The ego's stories are essentially complaints about the other person for not complying to our conditioning, fantasies, and desires. We paint the other person in a negative light, not necessarily because that person isn't right for us, but because he or she isn't fulfilling our ego's dreams and desires.

There's a big difference between being with the right person and being with the person our ego considers to be the right person. Many of us are with exactly the right person for us, but our egos don't think so! Is the ego right? What exposes the ego as an unworthy judge of who is right for us is that the ego finds fault with everyone after its idealizations have fallen away. Your ego will never be happy with who you are with, so basing your view of your partner on your ego's assessment isn't wise. The ego is in the business of judgment, not love.

Even when we find ourselves in a very difficult relationship, that relationship is the experience we are meant to have, for the time being anyway. Even an abusive relationship may be the experience we need to help us see that we don't deserve unloving treatment and to make sure we never put ourselves in that situation again. Every relationship we have leads to growth. We are changed by every one of our relationships, in a good way. We learn about ourselves, and we don't make the same mistakes again, which makes the next relationship more likely to be successful.

To get the most out of the relationship you are in, it won't be helpful to listen to the ego's stories about your partner or your relationship. They will only keep love from you. The ego's stories bring separation and conflict. Essence would tell a different story about your loved one than the one the ego tells. What might Essence's story be? It would probably be something like: "This person is in my life for me to love to the best of my ability. Let's see what happens if I try to do that." As Essence, we are meant to serve others and to serve life. The ego, on the other hand, is all about serving itself.

When we bring the demands and conditions of the ego into our relationships, love is undermined. It can't survive in an environment of judgments and demands. Love thrives when we accept others as they are, while allowing them to grow, develop, and be as they are meant to be. This is the kind of environment that we, as parents, would hope to provide our children. Being there for others, supporting their growth, supporting them in their trials, and celebrating life with them is a great service to others.

Other people are the companions that we (the Oneness) have given ourselves on this journey. If we listen to our ego, other people will feel more like our adversaries than like another aspect of our own true self. What if you really knew that every other person was an aspect of yourself, given to you to challenge and support you in your evolution—and given to you to love? It's up to every one of us to take the opportunity to love others and not to listen to the tales the ego spins.

UNNECESSARY THOUGHTS

It's obvious that some thoughts are unnecessary. Many of our thoughts come out of nowhere and have nothing to do with what we're doing or experiencing. We are like radio stations, picking up signals that come from who knows where, and some thoughts are like that: They come out of nowhere and seem to have little relevance to us personally. But even thoughts about our past and future don't contribute to what we are doing. Even thoughts about what we are doing aren't necessary!

How many of the thoughts you are having right now, or in any other moment, actually contribute to what you are doing and experiencing? When you examine this, you will discover that most thoughts don't contribute to your life, and they aren't needed to function. Try to find an example of a thought that is necessary. Necessary thoughts are few and far between.

Isn't it funny how important and necessary we think thinking is? This is part of the grand illusion. We think we need to think to make life happen and make it go smoothly. But when we examine the contribution our thoughts make to each moment, to our experience and to whatever we are doing, we discover not only that thoughts are unnecessary, but they also clutter the moment with confusion, negativity, and stress and therefore interfere with what we are experiencing and doing—and with our happiness. Our thoughts interfere with our happiness because they are so often demanding, pushy, or judgmental (e.g., "You have to get this done now!"). Such thoughts cause stress that can easily make us feel overwhelmed by life.

Life is never actually overwhelming because there's only so much we can do in a moment. But the mind brings ideas into the present moment about what we "have" to do, what we want to do, what we've done in the past, what others want us to do, whether we are able to do something, and ideas about any number of things unrelated to what we are doing or need to do. Such thoughts confuse and stress us out. They are not just unnecessary, but counterproductive. Stress makes us less effective and efficient, it makes us crabby and unhappy, and it's unhealthy. Those are the real results of giving our attention to thoughts and letting them guide our life.

The good news is that nearly all of our thoughts are unnecessary, not just a few of them. That makes discriminating between them much easier. We don't have to go sorting through our thoughts for the right ones. We just need to recognize that egoic thought belongs to the false self and is therefore false and not worthy of our attention. We can disregard all the thoughts that relate to *me* and *my story* and all the other chatter, judgments, opinions, memories, fantasies, dreams, desires, likes, dislikes, doubts, fears, complaints, and other negativity of the ego.

What we are left with is a functional mind that still knows how to read, calculate, use a computer, drive a car, follow a map or instructions, and do all the other things that the mind was designed for. The functional mind is something we use when we need it; it doesn't talk to us like the egoic mind. What a relief it is to realize that the voice in our head can be ignored! Can you trust this? Just start noticing how you don't need any of your thoughts to experience the present moment and to do what you need to do. See for yourself.

NOTICING THE IMPACT OF YOUR THOUGHTS

The world, without thoughts intervening, has a neutral or positive impact on us: When we look at the sky, we feel expanded (positive), unless the mind comes in with a complaint or judgment about the sky or something else. When we feel the breeze, we experience that (neutral), unless the mind comes in with a complaint or judgment about the breeze or something else. We get into trouble—negativity—when we encounter our egoic mind or other people's egoic minds. When the egoic mind mediates between us and experience, we generally suffer, because the ego tends to put a negative spin on our experience or take us out of an experience altogether.

Once we notice the impact the egoic mind has on our experience of life, we can learn to ignore our thoughts and notice the true impact of life. We can "step around" that mediator (the egoic mind) and choose to experience life as it actually is. If you encountered an unpleasant stranger, you would probably avoid that stranger. That's what we can do with our own and other people's egoic minds. We can step around or move beyond that interference to a place of peace, a place of no tension.

The way you know you are giving your attention to your egoic mind or someone else's is by the feeling of tension or stress created by doing that. When you feel tension, that's the time to step around that unpleasant intruder into reality, to step around that thought. Life itself is benign, but the ego makes life feel threatening or, at best, dull. The ego is either fending off its perceived difficulties and problems or trying to drum up some excitement, drama, and specialness. It doesn't know how to play the game of life simply; it opts for trouble and drama. But drama doesn't equal happiness, and simplicity and peace don't equal boredom. The ego has it backwards. It tries to create a happy life, and all it does is take us away from happiness.

To free ourselves from the egoic mind, all it takes is noticing the impact our thoughts have on our experience of life. Does the experience you are having cause you to contract and feel bad, or does a thought about the experience cause that contraction? This distinction is a big one. Once we see that it is only our thoughts that cause us to feel contracted and tense, we can become free from them. The only thing that keeps us tied to our thoughts, or imprisoned by them, is the belief that our thoughts belong to us and are therefore valid and necessary. They are not *your* thoughts, and they are not valid or necessary. When we finally see this, what a revelation it is, and so obvious really.

Every thought, except the most neutral or functional ones, such as, "this is a pencil" or "please pass the butter," has an impact on our consciousness, or energy. Every thought, except for functional ones, causes us to either contract or expand. Most of our thoughts cause us to contract because most are judgments. The ego tries to make itself feel superior by judging others, but the result of judging is always contraction. How interesting! And the best the ego can do to make us feel good is to come up with a fantasy of something we like. But fantasies actually result in contraction too. Anytime, the ego is in play, the result is contraction.

Thoughts that are uplifting and true are expressions, or reflections, of Essence. They cause us to feel spacious, expansive, and at peace. The truth feels good! This is a clue to what our true nature is like. When we are in touch with who we really are, we feel good, peaceful, content, and loving. That is why life without the mediation of the egoic mind feels good—because life *is* good, and our true nature is goodness. When we notice the impact of life on us in every moment without the intervention of the mind, we feel the excitement and joy of Essence. Who we really are is glad to be alive and grateful for everything it is experiencing through the character we are playing. That is the truth. When we learn to step around the egoic mind as it tries to intervene between us and life, we can finally be happy.

THE PRESENT HEALS

What heals the past? The old adage claims that time heals. If that's so, why does it heal, and is it really time that heals? Over time, our memories weaken and our ability and desire to bring the past into the present through thought weaken. Life starts getting in the way, as whatever was lost gets replaced by new life. That new life begins to get our attention more than what happened in the past. Time heals because life moves on to something new. Life brings us new experiences, opportunities, challenges, and relationships. Since we can only give our attention to one thought at a time, after some time has passed, our memories are naturally given less attention, they fade, and other thoughts take their place.

If this is how time heals, that is very good news, because that means we can speed the process of healing sorrows from the past and release ourselves from suffering over the past just by moving our attention away from thoughts about the past onto the present moment. Being in the Now is actually what heals old emotional wounds, not time. Shifting our attention to the present moment is not denying or repressing the past, but simply not creating unnecessary pain for ourselves. It is a very wise choice. We can continue to recreate, or reanimate, the pain of the past, or we can choose to leave the past in the past once we see that bringing memories into the present moment doesn't serve us, but only extends the pain and keeps us at a distance from life.

Putting our attention on anything other than our painful memories heals the past. Whatever we give our attention to becomes our experience. If we put our attention on the past, we will re-live the pain of the past and probably create more by telling ourselves upsetting stories, such as: "This shouldn't have happened." "If only I'd done something differently." "Why does this always happen to me?" By doing that, we create more pain for ourselves on top of whatever loss we had. That suffering isn't necessary. Dredging up memories and telling negative stories about the past isn't a healthy way to grieve, but a way we unknowingly increase our suffering and remove ourselves from the Now, where peace and happiness are available.

The past is a diluted memory, and the future is a figment of the ego's imagination. The past and future only exist as thoughts. The ego creates a sense of time through thoughts about the past and the future, and we can become entranced by the ego's world when we believe such thoughts *are* the past and future. What we imagine can seem very real, especially when those imaginations create feelings, which make our thoughts seem even more real. The painful feelings related to a loss often come more from what we tell ourselves about the loss than from the loss itself, especially the farther away in time we get from the loss.

There's a difference between grief and suffering unnecessarily over the past. Grief is a natural release of emotion over a loss, which takes time to adjust to. But many people grieve far beyond the time required to adjust to a loss because they continue to reinforce their pain by going over the past in their minds and telling themselves painful stories. Doing this isn't helpful and only prolongs the healing process.

Stopping this re-stimulation of pain by not giving our attention to memories or stories about the past heals the past and helps us move on to what life intends for us now. With every loss, come new possibilities. When we are present to anything other than our thoughts and feelings, we are likely to pick up on what life's intentions are for us and where life is leading us. Moreover, by being present to life as it is right now, we can discover the acceptance, joy, and excitement Essence has over being alive, even when life is challenging.

Life is always good, and we are always having the experience we need. If life doesn't seem that way, you are listening to the mind's sad or negative story about life. This kind of suffering is so unnecessary. When we drop out of our egoic mind and into this simple moment, we discover the truth about life. Life can be lived very well from this place of Presence, or being in the Now, because Presence is what's real, and the ego and its thoughts are not real. The good news is we have never needed the ego's thoughts to live our life, and therefore freedom from suffering is possible.

ESSENCE IS A FEELING OF HOME

"Home" is a very powerful word because everyone has an association with this word that runs very deep. You know the feeling of being Home when you experience it. "Home" has nothing to do with a house or with any other thing, but with our inner state. When we land in that place we recognize it, and we don't want to leave it; and yet, we do.

The feeling of being Home is all we have ever wanted, but often we don't stay there for long. Something always calls us away, and that is the mind—thoughts about something, anything. Instead of bringing us Home, our thoughts take us away from it. Our thoughts seem so important and necessary, and they are so enticing. Why must there be a dichotomy between what feels good and right and what seems necessary? The question is, necessary for whom? Who is it that calls us away from Home and why?

The ego is what calls us away from Home because it doesn't trust this place of calm, peace, safety, and completion. It doesn't trust being Home because it doesn't understand this place. It runs from the incomprehensible, the inexplicable, and what nourishes us, not because it doesn't want to be nourished, but because it doesn't trust that this place actually provides what it does. Do you trust this? When you finally rest and drop all striving and come Home, do you trust this place? Do you recognize it? Do you value it? Do you want to know how to spend more time there? Until you do trust this place, recognize it, value it, and desire to experience it, you won't stay there.

We are programmed to not trust being Home. Our conditioned self, the ego, tells us this place isn't trustworthy or valuable and that we should move on to something else, someplace else. The ego beckons us to travel somewhere else mentally or to get busy doing something—anything. The ego offers enticements away from Home and tries to convince us there is someplace or something to do that is even better than being Home.

It's not that there isn't a place in life for doing or that doing doesn't sometimes flow naturally out of this place of Home. But we all need to drop out of striving, planning, worrying, and fantasizing and just be Home sometimes, to nourish, recharge, and fortify ourselves and to inform our actions. Home is where the Heart is, and the Heart feels good. And God knows, we all need to feel good. We need Home like we need water and food, to sustain us in this difficult world.

We look for a sense of being Home in a physical home, in a family, in a lover. But unless we can experience it in the still moments of our life, no house, family, lover, or anything else will ever satisfy our longing for Home. The feeling of being Home is never found by doing, going somewhere, having things, or thinking, but by simply stopping and just *being* long enough to let ourselves feel that we are Home. Our longing for Home can call it forth. Know Home, value it, want it, and you will have it. The most precious attainment is right here in Stillness and in just being.

ABOUT THE AUTHOR

Gina Lake is a spiritual teacher who is devoted to helping others wake up and live in the Now through counseling, intensives, and her books. She has a masters degree in counseling psychology and over twenty years experience supporting people in their spiritual growth. Her books include *Radical Happiness, Embracing the Now, Anatomy of Desire, Return to Essence, What About Now? Loving in the Moment, Living in the Now,* and *Getting Free.* Her website offers information about her books and consultations, free e-books, book excerpts, a free monthly newsletter, a blog, and audio and video recordings: *www.radicalhappiness.com.*

Lightning Source UK Ltd.
Milton Keynes UK
29 March 2010

152057UK00002B/62/P